Lee Bailey's
Country Desserts

Lee Bailey's
Country Desserts

Cakes, Cookies, Ice Creams, Pies, Puddings & More

by Lee Bailey

✿

Photographs by Joshua Greene

Recipe Development and Research with Mardee Haidin Regan

GRAMERCY BOOKS
New York

For some reason simple country desserts make me think of children—
or of being a child. And my mother's older brother,
Edwin White, loved children more than any
man I have ever met. So this book is dedicated to my
Uncle Edwin's memory, with thanks to him for his part in
making my own childhood such a happy time.

This 1998 edition is published by Gramercy Books, a division of Random House Value Publishing, Inc., by arrangement with Clarkson N. Potter, Inc., a member of the Crown Publishing Group, 201 East 50th Street, New York, New York 10022.

Gramercy Books and colophon are trademarks of Random House Value Publishing, Inc.

Printed in China

Random House
New York • Toronto • London • Sydney • Auckland
http://www.randomhouse.com/

Library of Congress Cataloging-in-Publication Data

Bailey, Lee.
[Country desserts]
Lee Bailey's country desserts: cakes, cookies, ice creams, pies, puddings & more/by Lee Bailey; photographs by Joshua Greene; recipe development and research with Mardee Haidin Regan.
p.   cm.
Originally published: New York: Potter, ©1988.
Includes index.
ISBN 0-517-18749-3
1. Desserts.   I. Regan, Mardee Haidin.   II. Title.
TX773.B24   1988
641.8'6—dc21   97-23983
                                                                                                          CIP

Other Lee Bailey titles from Gramercy Books:

❀

LEE BAILEY'S COUNTRY WEEKENDS

LEE BAILEY'S COUNTRY FLOWERS

Contents

Introduction

Look, I'm not going to pretend I don't know that most of us have a sort of love-hate relationship with desserts. And, of course, I am also aware that some people with wills of steel are content with the likes of a nice red apple for dessert. But the truth is that when the rest of us are in the mood for a big, gooey concoction or a memory-nudging cobbler, a shiny apple just won't do the trick. And besides, what kind of celebration would it be if you served an apple with a candle stuck in it? Or an apple with a bride and groom on top? So I say full steam ahead, for there is always tomorrow to start the dubious rewards of periodic character-building restraint.

As you will see, this book is divided into chapters devoted to broad categories. This should not imply there is any particular pertinence to this arrangement—we could have just as easily started with "Cookies" as with "Ice Cream." So to get started, turn to the chapter that interests you most, and go backward and forward from there. I also suggest that you try making a few desserts you might never have attempted before—the summer pudding, for instance. One thing you can be sure of is that every recipe is simple, or certainly comparatively so.

Or, if you want to go for the easiest first, make the shortbread in the "Cookie" section, or the green tomato and apple tart in the "Pie" chapter, or the puréed mixed fruit ice in the "Ice Cream" section. Or flip to the "Coffee and Tea" chapter, and try the applesauce cake; it keeps wonderfully well and, considering what you get for your effort, is not hard to make, either. Another delicious and easy dessert is the honey custard (add a topping) in the "Pudding and Custard" chapter. For a gift, try the pecan or peanut brittle, which is even fun to make. And all the "Kids' Desserts" are especially uncomplicated.

If you have seen my other books you will be familiar with how I feel about "styling" food for photographs. It has always been my contention (and a point of contention, too!) that foods which have been fussed with too much before they are photographed come out looking a bit "holier than thou." And in a subtle—or maybe not-so-subtle—way they are a rebuke to the average cook. This is not to say I don't appreciate a beautiful dessert executed by a professional. Who wouldn't? I just don't think it is worth the time and effort to try to duplicate such perfection at home. As a hobby, yes; as a requisite, no.

This is merely a long-winded way to explain that you will come across some rather wonky-looking cakes and some less than perfectly crimped pie crusts here. These are absolutely swell as far as I am concerned—exactly as I want them to be. And I hope their down-home quality may actually encourage those of you who are a little doubtful about your cooking abilities.

When we were researching and collecting the recipes for Country Desserts, I wrote to members of my family, as well as to family friends, asking them to be on the lookout for old recipes and to send me their own favorites. And whenever I ran into friends whom I knew were particularly good cooks, I would ask for their help, too.

Later, after the book was almost completed, it occurred to me that this process of passing recipes from friend to friend and family to family, which I had been depending on, was how it was done years ago—before cookbooks were widely available.

Such recipe collections obviously were often part of a family's heritage, which a bride brought with her when she married. Maybe this is a romantic notion, but I find it gives many of these recipes, at least to me, a special appeal.

Of course, we did our share of tinkering with and changing the recipes as we went along, which I suppose is a cook's irresistible urge. And anyway, "customizing" recipes to suit one's preferences is in the spirit of collecting recipes, which ultimately become a part of one's own family heritage.

So aside from giving you a lot of delicious and easy desserts to choose from here, I hope this book will inspire you to do a bit of digging on your own. I'm sure there are a lot of old family favorites out there just waiting to be passed on. All you have to do is ask for them.

Here are some of the people I asked: With special thanks to Mardee Regan, who not only researched but tested endlessly and came up with her own observations and suggestions. She was with me on this project from the beginning right up to the final photographs. Long may she cook.

I might say the same to my famous Aunt Freddie and my Aunt Cora, as well as my Louisiana cousin, Mackie Kyle.

Grateful thanks, also, to all the other people who so generously contributed recipes (in alphabetical order): Mary Allen; Tom Booth and his family; Ruth Cashdollar; David Coltin; Joel English; André Fecteau; Jim Fobel and his Aunt Myra; Ina Garten; Carolyn Hart's mother, Eunice, and her Auntie Pearl; Lynn Grossman; Noel Harrington; Sherrye Henry; Pam Krausmann; Mrs. Yvonne LeBoeuf; Edna Lewis; Pam Lockard; Robert Mackintosh's mother, Anna, and his Aunt Irene; Mrs. Curtis McCaskill; John Prescott and his mother, Katherine; Gary Regan; Evelyne Slomon; Liz Smith and her mother, Mrs. Sloan Smith; and Jean Thackery.

And thanks to Sasha Clifton, who helped with the cooking when she could. Same to Petra Hanzlick and Kathy Flynn.

As always, thanks to Rochelle Udell and Doug Turshen—and to Julia and Benny.

And to all the people at Clarkson Potter—Carolyn Hart, Carol Southern, Gael Towey, Bruce Harris, Phyllis Fleiss, Sarah Wright, Susan Magrino, and Amy Schuler, to name a few—who just seem to keep on doing what they do so remarkably well.

To Joshua Greene, who took all these scrumptious-looking photographs. Boy, am I glad you did them and not me. I appreciate more than ever how hard it is to make things look simple and how well you do it.

Finally, to Carole Bannett, Joan Muli, and Tony Diaz—thanks for everything.

And as for you, Parker, what can I say?

It takes a heap of people to make a book out of an idea!

LEE BAILEY
Bridgehampton, Long Island

Applejack Ice
Berry Ice
Berry Ice Cream
Blood Orange Sherbet
Blowout Ice Cream
Bourbon-Pecan Ice Cream
Cantaloupe Ice
Chocolate-Chocolate Chip Ice Cream
Chocolate Nougat Ice Cream
Cinnamon Ice Cream
Eggless Vanilla-Bean Ice Cream
Espresso Ice
Espresso Ice Cream
Fig Ice Cream
Grape Ice
Grapefruit Ice
Honey and Honey-Roasted Peanut Ice Cream
Lemon Custard Ice Cream
Lime Ice
Maple-Black Walnut Ice Cream
Peach Pit Ice Cream
Peanut Brittle Ice Cream
Pear Ice
Peppermint Candy Ice Cream
Pineapple Sherbet
Pumpkin-Spice Custard Ice Cream
Rum-Raisin Ice Cream
Sugarless Fruit Ice
Toasted Coconut Ice Cream
Vanilla-Bean Custard Ice Cream
White House Ice Cream
Yogurt Ice Cream

Ice Cream and Ices

The very taste of rich, homemade custard ice cream, which as far as I am concerned is the quintessential summer country dessert, evokes in me the most teasingly pleasant of memories from long ago—warm evenings just when the light is disappearing and the day's heat relaxes its grip, an uncanny stillness as if time were holding its breath for a moment even as birds swoop and glide through the unmoving air in their twilight pursuit of insects. While these recollections are no match for Mr. Marcel P.'s thoughts at his famous first bite of the innocent little madeleine, I at least can appreciate how potent the connection sometimes is between taste and memory.

Even today in the small towns of Louisiana, the faithful sit down to the main meal on Sunday as soon after church as it can be put on the table. So it was when I was a boy. During the scorching days of summer, dessert at the end of this sumptuous lunch usually was ice cream when it was not fruit cobbler. Always custard based and often vanilla, the ice cream would occasionally be varied with the addition of seasonal berries and toppings. It would be served along with a variety of crisp little cookies or some marvelous generously frosted cake, which revealed its homemade origins in its slightly tilted angle.

Supper on these Sundays was apt to be a pickup affair, composed of leftovers and maybe one new dish. But not invariably. The best times were those when the ice cream and cake were not served at the end of the noontime meal, but were saved to be the *whole* supper that evening. Can you imagine how wonderful that was to a child? We didn't know how sinful such a thing would seem to most adults today. But on those blessed and innocent Sundays the trusty old hand-cranked ice-cream maker was set up on the back porch at about four in the afternoon, and the turning was begun. Children were given a shot at it first, while cranking was still easy. Then, as the custard began to freeze and the handle became more difficult to turn, the men took over. Kids were kept busy cracking the ice while also making a nuisance of themselves wanting to add more salt to the bucket and asking if the ice cream was ready yet. When the dasher was almost bound up by the thickening cream and the handle was almost impossible to turn, a large pan was brought out to hold the dasher as it was removed. Then a squabble usually ensued as we children fought to take the pan to the kitchen so we would have a taste, on the way, of what was clinging to the paddle. Meanwhile, the metal container was closed, with more ice packed on top to give the custard time to set and mature. When suppertime finally came, we children were allowed to eat as much ice cream and cake as we wanted. I suppose our parents figured that if we made ourselves sick, we would learn some kind of lesson—and, besides, the adults didn't show too much restraint themselves.

While I was growing up, this happy event usually occurred two or three times a year. I don't remember how or when the tradition ended, but I suppose people eventually got too diet conscious for it to go on forever. There is probably something to be said for being born too soon.

So there's a lot of ice cream in this chapter, along with variations and relatives: sherbets or sorbets, granités or ices, and a couple of hybrids like yogurt ice cream.

Incidentally, I always use an electric ice-cream freezer. I probably wouldn't bother today to hand-turn ice cream the way we did years ago. Of course, unlike today, at that time there weren't many places that sold good commercial ice cream, so if you wanted something really rich or special, you almost had to make it yourself. And, as you can tell from my recollections, the doing of it was a family affair —an entertainment that I doubt would go over in this electronic age.

If you don't own an electric ice-cream maker and you enjoy ice creams and ices, such a machine is a good investment and can be interesting to experiment with. You can make ice creams and ices from almost any kind of sweetened liquid or puréed fruit (or vegetable). And you might do as I have in the summer, when fruit is plentiful and cheaper: Make an essence of sugar and berries, freezing it to use later as a base for ices or for flavoring custard ice creams. The only caution in this case is not to go overboard. If you are like me, you will only use the fruit essence a couple of times during the winter. It won't be much of a saving or a convenience if, next spring, you have to throw out half of what you stashed away last summer because you never got around to using it.

At the end of the book I make some recommendations about available ice-cream makers and the advantages and drawbacks of the various kinds.

Elsewhere in the book are chapters on sauces and toppings to enhance the ice cream as well as recipes for cookies and cakes to make the whole occasion more festive. As a matter of fact, during the holidays years ago there often were dessert parties, which is an idea that might be fun to try again. Such a party affords a perfect excuse for you and your friends to indulge that sweet tooth. The fact that it is during the holidays helps salve the conscience.

Finally, if you haven't had much experience making ice cream and sherbets, note the proportions of milk, cream, sugar, and egg yolks in the various recipes as you try them. As you will see, some mixtures are cooked and others are not. The cooked mixtures usually have egg yolks to make a custard, and these are the richest kinds of ice cream. If this appeals to you, you can experiment using a basic custard, choosing any combination of eggs, cream, half-and-half, and milk, and then adding the flavoring in the form of fruit, spices, and so on. You can't go very wrong here.

Ices and sherbets generally are made without milk and sometimes include egg whites, but never yolks. These naturally have a lighter, icy texture.

Above, left to right: Eggless Vanilla-Bean Ice Cream; Cinnamon Ice Cream; Espresso Ice Cream; Chocoloate Nougat Ice Cream. *Below, left to right:* Fig Ice Cream; Grape Ice; Espresso Ice. *Opposite:* Grapefruit Ice

Chocolate Nougat Ice Cream

Here's an incredibly rich chocolate ice cream you'll love.

- 2 bars (3½ ounces) Tobler bittersweet chocolate, finely chopped
- 2 cups half-and-half
- ½ cup milk
- 3 large egg yolks, at room temperature
  Pinch of salt
- ⅔ cup sugar
- 1 teaspoon vanilla extract

Combine chopped chocolate, half-and-half, and milk in a medium saucepan. Cook, stirring, over low heat until chocolate melts and mixture is smooth, being careful not to scorch. Set aside.

Beat the egg yolks with the salt and sugar until sugar is dissolved. Add ½ cup of the chocolate mixture to the yolks to warm them, mix thoroughly, then add yolk mixture to the balance of the chocolate mixture. Return to heat and cook slowly, stirring all the while, until thick enough to coat a spoon, about 2 minutes.

Stir in vanilla off the heat and allow to cool.

Pour mixture into an ice-cream maker and freeze according to manufacturer's directions.

Makes approximately 1 quart

Cinnamon Ice Cream

I think cinnamon must be everyone's favorite spice. If you like it, this is your ice cream. Serve it with a simple tea cake or crisp vanilla wafers.

- 1½ cups heavy cream
- 1½ cups milk
- 2½ tablespoons fresh ground cinnamon, or 3 tablespoons finely chopped cinnamon sticks
- ½ teaspoon ground cloves or ginger
  Pinch of salt

Combine all ingredients in a large, heavy saucepan and cook over low heat, stirring, just until bubbles start to form around the edges. Cover and cool to room temperature. When cooled, strain and refrigerate until well chilled. Pour mixture into an ice-cream maker and freeze according to manufacturer's directions.

Makes approximately 1½ pints

Eggless Vanilla-Bean Ice Cream

This eggless ice cream is for people who don't like their ice cream too custardy. It's surprisingly easy to make and very tasty.

- 3 cups half-and-half
- ½ cup sugar
- 1 vanilla bean, split and cut into several pieces

Mix the half-and-half with the sugar in a large saucepan and scald over low heat, being sure that all the sugar dissolves and that the mixture does not scorch. Add the vanilla bean and allow to cool completely. Refrigerate for several hours, then strain to remove vanilla pods. Scrape any remaining vanilla seeds into the mixture, then pour into an ice-cream maker and freeze according to manufacturer's directions.

Makes about 1½ pints

Espresso Ice

Espresso ice is served all around Italy, so you have probably had it before. If you haven't, now is the time. Sometimes it is made by combining coffee and simple syrup, but here it is made with sweetened coffee, which I like better.

- 3 cups hot, fresh, strong coffee
- 3 tablespoons sugar
- 3 strips orange peel about ½ inch wide (optional)
  Whipped cream flavored with a liqueur
  Powdered instant espresso

While coffee is still hot, stir in the sugar and add the orange peel. Allow the mixture to cool, then refrigerate, covered, until well chilled. Remove peel.

Pour mixture into an ice-cream maker and freeze according to manufacturer's directions.*

Serve with flavored or spiked whipped cream on top, sprinkled with a little powdered espresso.

Makes about 1½ pints

* This is also easy to make in the freezer compartment of your refrigerator. Pour the finished coffee mixture into metal ice-cube trays (without dividers) or any one-quart metal container. Return to freezer compartment and let freeze, stirring or puréeing it at intervals as it freezes, to break up ice crystals.

Espresso Ice Cream

This is a variation on coffee ice cream but with a stronger flavor. It is also as rich as espresso ice is light.

2 cups heavy cream
1 cup milk
5 large egg yolks, at room temperature
⅔ cup superfine sugar
1 teaspoon vanilla extract
1 tablespoon powdered instant espresso, plus extra for sprinkling on top

Combine the cream and milk in a large saucepan and bring just to a boil over high heat, stirring all the while. Set aside.

Whisk together the egg yolks and sugar until frothy. Gradually add the hot mixture, whisking, until well mixed. Pour back into the saucepan and cook over moderate heat until mixture coats a spoon and is thickened, about 2 minutes. Do not overcook.

Stir in the vanilla and powdered espresso. Place cling wrap directly onto the surface of the cream. Allow to cool to room temperature. Chill mixture.

Pour mixture into ice-cream maker and freeze according to manufacturer's directions.

Serve with additional powdered espresso sprinkled on top.

Makes approximately 1½ pints

Fig Ice Cream

This recipe is an old one from Louisiana, where there is an endless supply of fresh figs in early summer. The ice cream has a delightful and subtle flavor.

1 cup sugar
¼ cup water
1 tablespoon distilled white vinegar
Pinch of salt
2 large egg whites, stiffly beaten
4 cups crushed fresh figs
1½ cups milk

Combine the sugar, water, vinegar, and salt in a saucepan. Over moderate heat, boil rapidly to the thread stage, 230 degrees on a candy thermometer.

Pour mixture in a thin stream into the beaten egg whites and then combine with figs. Stir in milk.

Pour mixture into an ice-cream maker and freeze according to manufacturer's directions.

Makes 1 to 1½ quarts

Grape Ice

Don't use seedless grapes for this; grapes with seeds have much better flavor.

2 cups white grape juice
½ cup sugar
1½ pounds wine or red concord grapes, stemmed
3 tablespoons fresh lemon juice, or to taste

Combine the grape juice and sugar in a medium saucepan and simmer over low heat until the sugar dissolves and mixture is clear, about 5 minutes.

Meanwhile, purée grapes in a food processor. Push mixture through a sieve to remove skins and seeds, then stir grape purée and lemon juice into grape juice mixture and chill.

Pour mixture into an ice-cream maker and freeze according to manufacturer's directions.

Makes approximately 1½ pints

Grapefruit Ice

This is infinitely tastier than the ubiquitous lemon ice.

½ to 1 medium grapefruit, unpeeled
½ cup superfine sugar
1½ cups water
2 teaspoons fresh lemon juice
1 large egg white, beaten to soft peaks
Vodka (optional)

Squeeze out 2 tablespoons juice from the grapefruit and set aside. Cut the grapefruit into ½-inch pieces (for about 1½ cups) and put into a saucepan with just enough water to cover. Over low heat, boil slowly until tender, about 10 minutes. Drain, discarding the water. Combine grapefruit with 3 tablespoons of the sugar and purée in a food processor.

In a medium saucepan, combine remaining sugar and the water. Stir over low heat until sugar dissolves. Remove and allow to cool, then freeze for 10 to 15 minutes. Meanwhile, simmer grapefruit purée until thick, about 15 to 20 minutes. Make sure it doesn't scorch. Stir in grapefruit and lemon juices and the sugar syrup and chill. Just before freezing, fold in egg white.

Pour the mixture into an ice-cream maker and freeze according to manufacturer's directions.

If desired, make an indentation on the top of each scoop with a tablespoon and fill with vodka.

Makes about 1 quart

Above: Peach Pit Ice Cream; Maple-Black Walnut Ice Cream   _Below:_ Honey and Honey-Roasted Peanut Ice Cream; Pear Ic

Above: Peanut Brittle Ice Cream; Lime Ice   *Below:* Lemon Custard Ice Cream; Peppermint Candy Ice Cream

Honey and Honey-Roasted Peanut Ice Cream

The person who thought up honey-roasted peanuts must have had me in mind. I love them. Here they are added to honey ice cream—a marriage made in heaven.

   1 cup heavy cream
   1 cup milk
  ⅔ cup honey
   3 large egg yolks, at room temperature
      Pinch of salt
   1 cup coarsely chopped honey-roasted peanuts

Combine the cream and milk in a medium saucepan. Cook slowly over moderate heat until heated through, about 2 minutes. Off the heat, add the honey and mix until completely dissolved. Set aside.

    Beat the egg yolks with the salt until frothy, then add ½ cup of the honey-cream mixture to heat the yolks. Return saucepan to low heat and add warmed yolks. Stirring all the while, cook until the mixture coats the back of a spoon.

    Remove from heat and allow to cool before stirring in peanuts. Chill mixture.

    Pour mixture into an ice-cream maker and freeze according to manufacturer's directions.

Makes approximately 1½ pints

Lime Ice

Another easy recipe, with a little bite.

  1 to 1½ cups fresh lime juice (or a combination of lime and lemon)
  3 cups simple syrup (made from 3 cups each sugar and water, heated until mixture is clear and sugar is dissolved)
     Grated zest of 1 lemon

Combine 1 cup of the juice with the simple syrup. Since lime juice is very tart, add juice carefully until you get a balance you like. (Remember that when the mixture is frozen it will not taste as sweet as it does at this stage.) Stir in grated zest, pour mixture into an ice-cream maker, and freeze according to manufacturer's directions.

Makes 2½ pints

Maple-Black Walnut Ice Cream

This recipe couldn't be simpler, and it is a good way to use up some of that maple syrup that we all seem to be given as gifts.

   2 cups half-and-half
  ¾ cup good-quality maple syrup
   1 cup coarsely chopped black walnuts

Combine the half-and-half and maple syrup in a medium bowl and mix well. Add the walnuts.

    Pour into an ice-cream maker and freeze according to manufacturer's directions.

Makes approximately 1½ pints

Peach Pit Ice Cream

This unusual recipe makes a delicious ice cream with a strong peachy flavor.

 1¼ pounds ripe unblemished peaches (about 8 large)
  ¼ cup fresh lemon juice
 1½ cups heavy cream
 1½ cups milk
  ¾ cup sugar
   3 large egg yolks, at room temperature

Peel and pit peaches, reserving peach skins and pits. In a food processor or blender, purée peach flesh with the lemon juice. You should have about 2¼ cups of purée. Cover and refrigerate.

    Place skins and pits in a large saucepan along with the cream and milk. Simmer, covered, over low heat for 20 minutes, being careful not to let mixture boil. It may look slightly separated because of the acid in the fruit, but don't worry. Stir in sugar to dissolve and remove from the heat. Whisk yolks and add about ½ cup of the hot liquid to warm them. Mix well and pour warmed yolks into the hot mixture, stirring constantly. Return saucepan to the heat and cook until custard coats the back of a spoon, about 8 minutes. Again, be careful not to let mixture boil; boiling may cause custard to curdle.

    Press a sheet of wax paper or cling wrap directly onto the surface of the mixture and allow to cool. When cool, strain and combine with the fruit pulp. Mix and chill.

    Pour mixture into an ice-cream maker and freeze according to manufacturer's directions.

Makes about 1 quart

Pear Ice

What a marvelously refreshing flavor this has. By all means, give it a try.

1½ cups pear purée (made from 3 ripe medium pears, peeled and cored)
1½ cups simple syrup (made from 1½ cups each sugar and water, heated until sugar is dissolved—less sugar to taste)
1 tablespoon fresh lemon juice
Pear brandy (optional)

In a large bowl, mix pear purée, simple syrup, and lemon juice, pour into an ice-cream maker, and freeze according to manufacturer's directions.

If desired, to serve, make an indentation in the top of each scoop of ice with the back of a tablespoon and fill with a tablespoon of pear brandy.

Makes about 1½ to 2 pints

Peppermint Candy Ice Cream

Peppermint candy ice cream was a great favorite of my grandmother's, so I had it many times when I was growing up. It was usually served with the great Intermont white cake on page 42.

2 cups half-and-half
3½ ounces red-and-white striped peppermint candies, crushed until fine with a hammer or rolling pin
½ cup superfine sugar

Scald the half-and-half in a large saucepan over medium heat, then remove from heat. While still hot, add the candy and sugar. Stir until candy and sugar are dissolved. Allow to cool, then chill.

Pour mixture into an ice-cream maker and freeze until firm according to manufacturer's directions.

Makes approximately 1½ pints

Peanut Brittle Ice Cream

There is a recipe for nut brittle on page 147, which you could substitute for the peanut brittle in this recipe. Incidentally, if you have never made brittle before, you will be surprised how very easy it is. And how good.

2 cups half-and-half
⅔ cup firmly packed light brown sugar
3 tablespoons light corn syrup
3 large egg yolks, at room temperature
2 teaspoons vanilla extract
1 cup coarsely chopped or broken peanut brittle

Combine the half-and-half, brown sugar, and corn syrup in a medium saucepan and cook over medium heat, stirring all the while, until the sugar dissolves completely. Remove from heat.

Beat egg yolks until creamy, then add ½ cup of the hot cream mixture, stirring to heat them. Put saucepan back on heat and add the warmed yolks, stirring. Continue to cook over medium-low heat until mixture coats the spoon.

Remove from heat, allow to cool, and stir in vanilla. Chill and pour into an ice-cream maker, freeze until partially set, about 20 minutes. Stir in peanut brittle and continue freezing until firm, following manufacturer's directions.

Makes approximately 1 quart

Lemon Custard Ice Cream

Almost everyone knows about lemon sherbet and lemon ice, but what about lemon ice cream? It has a flavor and texture all its own and, although richer than ice or sherbet, is equally refreshing.

⅔ cup sugar
2½ cups half-and-half
5 large egg yolks, at room temperature
Grated zest of 1 large lemon
½ cup fresh lemon juice

Combine the sugar and half-and-half in a large saucepan and cook over low heat until sugar dissolves, stirring all the while. Set aside.

Beat the egg yolks until creamy, then add ½ cup of the cream to warm them. Return cream mixture to medium-low heat and stir in the warmed yolks. Cook until the mixture coats the back of a spoon, about 5 minutes.

Off the heat, stir in the zest and lemon juice. Mix well and allow to cool. Chill.

Pour mixture into an ice-cream maker and freeze according to manufacturer's directions.

Makes approximately 1½ pints

Blowout Ice Cream

Berry Ice Cream

Chocolate-Chocolate Chip Ice Cream

Bourbon-Pecan Ice Cream

Clockwise from left:
Applejack Ice;
Cantaloupe Ice;
Blood Orange Sherbet;
Berry Ice

Berry Ice Cream

Like berry ice, an ice cream may be made with just about any ripe berry, either with the seeds and pulp or just pulp alone. Here it is made with strawberries.

    6   tablespoons sugar
    1½   teaspoons all-purpose flour
         Pinch of salt
    1   cup half-and-half
    1   large egg, lightly beaten
    1   cup milk
    1   teaspoon vanilla extract
    1   pint fresh strawberries, washed, hulled,
         and crushed

Mix the sugar, flour, and salt in the top of a double boiler. Stir in the half-and-half, then cook over boiling water for about 5 minutes, stirring all the while. Cover and continue cooking over boiling water for 10 minutes longer. Remove from heat and spoon a little of the hot mixture into the beaten egg to heat it. Add the warmed egg to the milk and return double boiler to the heat.

Place mixture over hot, not boiling, water and stir constantly until mixture coats a spoon, about 5 minutes. Strain and chill.

When cold, stir in the milk, vanilla, and berries.

Pour mixture into an ice-cream maker and freeze according to manufacturer's directions.

Makes about 1½ pints

Bourbon-Pecan Ice Cream

This is a nice southern variation on an old favorite combination. The pecans and bourbon could also be added to a simple custard ice cream.

    2½   cups half-and-half
    ⅓   cup firmly packed light brown sugar
    ⅓   cup granulated sugar
    1   cup coarsely chopped pecans
    2   to 3 tablespoons bourbon

Combine the half-and-half with the sugars in a small saucepan. Slowly heat until sugars dissolve, then set aside to cool. Stir in the pecans and bourbon, then pour into an ice-cream maker and freeze until firm, according to manufacturer's directions.

Makes approximately 1½ pints

Berry Ice

Almost any variety of berry can be used here, with or without the seeds and pulp, sweetened to taste. You should remember, however, that freezing diminishes the sweetness of the mixture, so it should taste a little sweeter before freezing than you might like.

    3½   cups fresh raspberries
    2   tablespoons fresh lemon juice
    1   cup ice water
    ½   to ¾ cup superfine sugar, depending on
         sweetness of berries
    2   large egg whites, beaten to soft peaks

In a food processor or blender, purée berries with the lemon juice, then set aside. Mix water and sugar in a small saucepan and set over low heat, stirring until sugar is dissolved. Let cool. Combine purée and sugar mixture and mix well. Fold in egg whites. Pour the mixture into an ice-cream maker and freeze until firm, according to manufacturer's directions.

Makes about 1½ pints

Chocolate-Chocolate Chip Ice Cream

For all you chocolate freaks—what a way to go!

    ½   cup sugar
    8   ounces semisweet chocolate, coarsely
         chopped
    2½   cups half-and-half
         Pinch of salt
    1½   teaspoons vanilla extract
    1   cup semisweet chocolate chips

Place sugar in a food processor and process until finely ground, about 20 seconds. Add chopped chocolate and process until chocolate and sugar form small pellets.

Meanwhile, bring half-and-half just to a boil in a small saucepan over medium heat. When hot, pour into the processor and process until sugar and chocolate are melted.

Pour mixture into a bowl and add salt and vanilla. Allow to cool slightly, then stir in chocolate chips. Chill thoroughly, then freeze in an ice-cream maker according to manufacturer's directions.

Makes approximately 1 quart

Applejack Ice

Eating applejack ice is like having a crisp, icy-cold apple with just a little kick of brandy. Delicious after a rich meal.

> 1½ cups unsweetened applesauce
> 1½ cups unsweetened apple juice
> 3⅓ cups superfine sugar
> ¼ cup fresh lemon juice
> ¼ cup applejack (apple brandy)
>
> **Garnish**
> Cinnamon sticks or ground cinnamon

In a large bowl, stir together the applesauce, apple juice, sugar, and lemon juice. Strain, if desired, through a fine sieve. Pour the mixture into an ice-cream maker and freeze until somewhat firm, about 20 minutes. Pour in the applejack and freeze until firm, according to the manufacturer's directions.

Serve garnished with a cinnamon stick or with a light sprinkling of cinnamon over the top.

Makes approximately 1½ pints

Blowout Ice Cream

This is one of those ice-cream concoctions that you might want to experiment with. Use this recipe as a guide for making your own madness. Anything goes!

> 1 recipe Vanilla-Bean Custard Ice Cream (page 18)
> 4 to 8 Outrageous Brownies (page 138), cut into chunks or crumbled
> ½ cup coarsely chopped honey-roasted peanuts
> 2 teaspoons powdered instant espresso (optional)
> ½ cup semisweet chocolate chips (optional)
> 2 tablespoons bourbon or coffee-flavored liqueur (optional)

Follow the directions for making the ice cream. When the mixture is frozen almost solid, remove the freezing canister and fold in any or all of the remaining ingredients. Spoon into a container and freeze until solid, at least 3 hours.

Makes 1 to 1½ quarts, depending on what you add

Cantaloupe Ice

This is about as easy as an ice can be—and delicious. Just make sure to use a vine-ripened cantaloupe.

> ⅔ cup sugar
> ⅔ cup water
> 3½ cups puréed cantaloupe (about 1 large melon)
> 1 tablespoon fresh lemon juice

Combine sugar and water in a small saucepan. Heat just long enough to dissolve sugar. Allow to cool and refrigerate this "simple syrup."

In a large bowl, combine puréed cantaloupe with the lemon juice and chill along with the simple syrup. Chill both fruit and syrup for about an hour.

Combine fruit and syrup and place in an ice-cream maker and freeze according to manufacturer's directions.

Makes about 1½ pints

Blood Orange Sherbet

When sliced, blood oranges are one of the most beautiful fruits because of the color variations in any particular batch. They are marvelous simply peeled, sliced, and sprinkled with sugar, but try a scoop of blood orange sherbet with them for a real treat.

> ⅓ cup sugar
> 1 cup water
> 2 cups strained blood orange juice
> 2 teaspoons fresh lemon juice
> 2 tablespoons finely grated blood orange zest
> 2 tablespoons orange-flavored liqueur or vodka (optional)
> 3 large egg whites, beaten until stiff

Combine the sugar and water in a small saucepan and heat until sugar is melted and mixture is clear. Remove and chill.

In a glass bowl, combine the chilled sugar syrup, orange juice, lemon juice, zest, and liqueur. Mix thoroughly, then fold in the egg whites using an over-and-under motion. Continue folding until no egg white streaks remain in the mixture.

Pour mixture into an ice-cream maker and freeze until firm, according to manufacturer's directions.

Makes approximately 1½ pints

Top, left and right:
Pineapple Sherbet;
Toasted Coconut Ice Cream
Above:
Sugarless Fruit Ice
Right: Pumpkin-Spice
Custard Ice Cream

Right: Vanilla-Bean
Custard Ice Cream
Below: Yogurt Ice Cream
Bottom, left and right:
Rum-Raisin Ice Cream;
White House Ice Cream

Pineapple Sherbet

Undoubtedly you've had pineapple sherbet many times, but if you have never had it made with shredded fresh pineapple, you have a treat in store.

- 1 large pineapple, trimmed and cored, the flesh shredded with a fork (approximately 2 cups pineapple flesh)
- 1 cup unsweetened pineapple juice
- ⅔ to 1⅓ cups superfine sugar (depending on the sweetness of pineapple)
- 3 tablespoons fresh lemon juice
  Rum

Taste pineapple to judge its sweetness, so you will know about how much sugar you will want to use.

Combine pineapple juice with desired amount of sugar in a medium saucepan. Heat, stirring, until all the sugar is dissolved. Allow to cool slightly, then add the lemon juice and fresh pineapple. Add more sugar if mixture is too tart. (And remember, once frozen, mixture will taste less sweet.) Allow to cool, then chill.

Pour mixture into an ice-cream maker and freeze until firm according to manufacturer's directions.

Top with a bit of rum, if desired, when serving.

Makes approximately 1½ pints

Sugarless Fruit Ice

This sort of dessert is perfect when you are pressed by time and your diet. Fruit ice is fast and sugarless.

- 2 packages (10 ounces each) mixed frozen fruit, almost thawed
- ⅔ cup chilled unsweetened apple juice or ice water
- 2 tablespoons *eau-de-vie* or fruit-flavored brandy (optional)

Purée almost-thawed fruit in a food processor or blender, then stir in apple juice.

Pour mixture into an ice-cream maker and freeze until almost firm. If you are using *eau-de-vie*, add it now; if not, continue freezing until firm according to manufacturer's directions.

Makes approximately 1½ pints

Rum-Raisin Ice Cream

Another time, you can vary this recipe by using dried figs instead of dark raisins.

- 1 cup dark raisins
- ⅓ cup dark rum
- 2½ cups half-and-half
- ⅔ cup firmly packed light brown sugar
- ½ teaspoon ground cinnamon

Many hours ahead, or even the night before, mix the raisins and rum and let raisins soak until the liquid is absorbed.

Combine the half-and-half and brown sugar in a large saucepan and simmer over low heat, stirring, until sugar is dissolved. Let cool, then stir in cinnamon. Chill.

Just before freezing, stir in raisins, reserving any rum that was not absorbed.

Pour mixture into an ice-cream maker and freeze until almost firm. If you have any leftover rum, add it now. Otherwise, continue freezing until firm according to manufacturer's directions.

Makes approximately 1½ pints

Vanilla-Bean Custard Ice Cream

This is the real thing, rich as all get out with cream and eggs and the custard flecked with vanilla seeds. If you like vanilla, here is the granddaddy of them all.

- 1 cup milk
- ⅔ cup sugar
- 2 vanilla beans, cut in half lengthwise
- 9 large egg yolks, at room temperature
- 2 cups heavy cream

Combine the milk, sugar, and vanilla beans in the top of a double boiler and heat over barely simmering water. Lightly beat the yolks. When milk mixture is almost to the point of boiling, pour a little into the yolks to warm them. Stir and add a bit more hot milk.

Pour warmed yolks into the milk in a slow, steady stream, stirring all the while. Continue to cook, stirring constantly, over hot, not boiling, water until mixture coats the spoon.

Press a sheet of wax paper or cling wrap directly onto the surface of the custard and allow to cool to room temperature.

Add cream to the custard and refrigerate for several hours.

Just before freezing, remove vanilla beans and scrape their seeds into the mixture. Stir and pour into an ice-cream maker and freeze according to manufacturer's directions.

Makes 1 quart

Toasted Coconut Ice Cream

Toasting improves the taste of coconut immeasurably—and I am especially partial to using it that way. This mixture is uncooked, unless you call toasting the coconut cooking, so it is very simple to prepare.

1¼ cups canned cream of coconut
1 cup milk
½ cup heavy cream
Pinch of salt
1 cup shredded fresh coconut, toasted,* plus additional for serving

Combine the cream of coconut, milk, and cream in a large bowl. Sprinkle salt over mixture and whisk until well mixed. Sprinkle toasted coconut over all and gently fold in.

Pour the mixture into an ice-cream maker and freeze until firm according to manufacturer's directions. Serve with additional toasted coconut on top if desired.

Makes approximately 1½ pints

* To toast the coconut, spread on a jelly-roll pan and place in a preheated 375-degree oven. Toast until it turns golden, stirring around occasionally with a large fork.

Pumpkin-Spice Custard Ice Cream

Use the basic recipe for the filling for pumpkin chiffon pie, page 106, but add a cup of milk to the finished custard to make it more liquid. Mix well and chill.

Pour mixture into an ice-cream maker, then freeze until firm according to manufacturer's directions.

You might also make an ice-cream pie, using this ice-cream filling in the gingersnap crust instead of the regular filling.

Makes approximately 1 quart

White House Ice Cream

Obviously, this is so named because of the "George Washington" cherries used to flavor it. Only we switched and used dried sour Michigan cherries; see page 83 for the source if you don't find them in your local market.

4 ounces dried sour Michigan cherries
½ cup kirsch
2½ cups half-and-half
½ cup sugar
1 vanilla bean, split lengthwise
4 large egg yolks, at room temperature

Mix the cherries and the kirsch and soak for several hours, preferably overnight. Cover and set aside.

Combine the half-and-half, sugar, and vanilla bean in a large saucepan. Over low heat, cook until sugar is dissolved and bubbles begin to form around the edge of the pot.

Whisk the egg yolks until creamy, then add ½ cup of the heated cream to warm the yolks. Pour warmed yolks into the cream and continue to cook, stirring, until mixture coats the back of a spoon.

Remove saucepan from heat and take out the vanilla bean. Scrape vanilla seeds into the custard and mix. Allow to cool completely, then chill. Just before freezing, add cherries and any leftover kirsch to cream.

Pour mixture into an ice-cream maker and freeze until firm according to manufacturer's directions.

Makes approximately 1½ pints

Yogurt Ice Cream

You can vary the flavor of this recipe by using a different kind of frozen juice concentrate—or you can make a combination of juices.

4 cups vanilla yogurt
⅔ cup frozen tangerine juice concentrate, thawed

Combine the yogurt and concentrate in a large bowl and mix thoroughly.

Pour into an ice-cream maker and freeze until firm according to manufacturer's directions.

Makes approximately 1 quart

Cakes

Previous page, clockwise from left: Banana Layer Cake; Blackberry Cake; German Chocolate Cake; Devil's Food Cake with Chocolate Buttercream Icing; Brown Sugar Glazed Cake

Maybe it's my imagination, but I have the feeling that people don't make cakes the way they used to. Am I right? Was it the advent of those cake mixes, or did people simply start thinking that making cakes from scratch just wasn't worth the trouble—or that there really wasn't enough difference anyway? Well, whatever, I'd like to see the trend reversed.

It seems to me I know an awful lot of good cooks nowadays who have never even thought of baking a cake. As someone who has been making them off and on for forty years, I can say from experience that cakes are among the simplest desserts to put together.

The very idea of taking the time to stir up one of those unimaginative cake mixes, when you only have to spend a few extra minutes to create something really special, makes me see red. Granted, the first time you try, you will probably bumble around a bit, but after that, making cakes will be a snap.

When you think about it, cake making is only a matter of creaming the shortening and sugar, stirring in the eggs, mixing and sifting the dry ingredients, and then adding them, alternating with a liquid. Now I ask you, does that sound so difficult? Incidentally, when I sift dry ingredients together, I do so on sheets of wax paper instead of plates. It's easier to handle, and there's no washing up afterward. And I always sift flour for cakes *before* measuring it.

There isn't a cake mix around that can come even near my Aunt Cora's "special occasion" Intermont white cake on page 42. And see how uncomplicated that recipe is.

If you are worried about making a boiled icing (frosting), then don't. Put the cake together with a flavored buttercream mixture instead. Or simply substitute whipped cream and fruit, as for the fresh peach cake on page 38.

Aunt Cora was the cake maker in our family. What beauties she would turn out! I used to watch her make boiled frosting without using a candy thermometer, and it always seemed to come out just right—not too sugary and never too runny. I admit I've never quite mastered the technique without the thermometer, although she did try to show me how. For the record, the other two family favorites were her banana cake and her coconut cake.

Over the years, I remember having at one time or another some version of almost all the cakes in this chapter, but it was the Intermont, the coconut, and the banana cakes that keep coming back again and again.

There aren't any real secrets to cake making if you give yourself the time to think out what you are doing. Make sure your oven racks are level and the oven temperature is correct. Use an oven thermometer if you are in doubt. Sift the ingredients together properly, and always measure carefully. These certainly are minimal demands.

When mixing, start with butter that is slightly softened, and beat it with the sugar until the sugar is dissolved and the mixture is fluffy; I use an electric hand mixer for this. Beat in eggs quickly but thoroughly, one at a time.

When adding the dry ingredients, alternate dry with liquid, starting and ending with the dry, which you add in 3 or 4 portions. The batter must be well mixed, but not overmixed.

If the recipe calls for separating the egg whites and beating them before they are added to the batter, fold these in last. To fold in whites properly, don't go at it in too vigorous a manner. Dump beaten whites on the batter and, using a rubber spatula and a light touch, start folding them in with a rolling over-and-under motion, revolving the bowl at the same time. Continue only until there are no more streaks of beaten white showing. Don't overdo this mixing either.

Pour the batter into prepared pans. If you are worried about sticking, line the bottoms of the greased pans with wax paper and then oil and lightly flour the whole inside, including the paper.

To bake, place the pans side by side but not touching on the same shelf, if possible. If they must go one in back of the other or on two different shelves, quickly reverse them halfway through the cooking time.

If you are uncertain of the cooking time, test the cakes with a cake tester or straw several times toward the end of what you *think* is the proper cooking time. Make sure the cake does not overcook; overcooking will dry out the cake. When done, the layers should have pulled away slightly from the sides of the pans, and the tester should come out with no uncooked batter clinging to it.

Let the cake layers or tube cake cool somewhat before inverting onto a cooling rack. And before inverting, loosen the edges gently with a knife. Once the cake is out of the pan, allow it to cool completely before icing it—or before wrapping it, if you are going to ice the cake later.

I always brush the cake lightly with a pastry brush to remove any crumbs. By doing this, the frosting will adhere better and not pull away from the sides as it is applied.

When stacking cake layers, hold them in place with a couple of toothpicks. If you are leery of icing the whole cake—that is, the sides as well as the top—then only fill between the layers, secure them with toothpicks, and pile the frosting on top, letting it move down the sides with a minimum of urging. If the frosting is the correct consistency, and it *will* be if you use a candy thermometer, it will move very slowly. If it runs off quickly, keep piling it back on top until it sets properly. The less you try to control a boiled icing as it cools, the more natural and attractive it will be. Of course, this tip is for cooked icings; buttercream frosting must be spread with a knife, dipped in water if necessary, or a metal or rubber spatula.

Be the first on your block to reverse the anti-cake making trend, and rediscover its pleasures and rewards. You won't be sorry.

Above: Banana Layer Cake. *Below:* Blueberry Buckle

Above: Blackberry Cake. *Below:* Brown Sugar Glazed Cake

Blackberry Cake

Jean Thackery, who says a version of this cake has been a family standby for years, sent this to me. Its dense texture makes it a good choice to take along on picnics, where the food may get a bit of rough handling. At home try it with rich vanilla ice cream or, if you really want to go wild, top it with ice cream and blackberry sauce.

- ½ cup (1 stick) unsalted butter, softened
- 1 cup firmly packed light brown sugar
- 3 large eggs, separated, at room temperature
- 2 cups sifted cake flour (not self-rising)
- ½ teaspoon baking soda
- 2 teaspoons baking powder
- 1 teaspoon grated nutmeg
- ¼ teaspoon ground cloves
- ½ teaspoon ground cinnamon
- 1 cup seedless blackberry jam
- ⅓ cup sour cream
  Confectioners' sugar

Preheat the oven to 375 degrees. Line the bottom of a lightly greased 9-inch tube pan with a piece of wax paper cut to fit.

Cream the butter and brown sugar until fluffy, about 3 minutes. Add the yolks and mix well.

Sift the dry ingredients together. Stir the jam into the sour cream. Add the dry mixture to the creamed mixture, alternating with the sour cream. Beat the egg whites until stiff, then fold in with an over-and-under motion. Pour batter into pan and bake for 45 to 50 minutes. Allow cake to cool slightly, then run a knife around the edge of the pan and turn out onto a cooling rack. Remove wax paper.

Place a cake rack or doily over the top of the cake and sprinkle confectioners' sugar over it to create a pattern.

Serves 12

Banana Layer Cake

My Aunt Cora first made this cake and then, as her recipe was passed around, most other family members followed suit.

Lighter than banana bread, it uses fresh bananas between the layers. These are fairly perishable, but in our case the cake never lasted long enough for that to make much difference.

- 2½ cups sifted cake flour (not self-rising)
- 2½ teaspoon baking powder
- ½ teaspoon baking soda
  Pinch of ground cloves
- 1¼ teaspoons ground cinnamon
- ½ teaspoon grated nutmeg
- ½ teaspoon salt
- 1¼ cups sugar
- ½ cup (1 stick) unsalted butter, softened
- 2 large eggs
- 1 teaspoon vanilla extract
- 1½ cups mashed ripe bananas
  Several bananas for filling, sliced lengthwise
  Additional sugar for filling

Boiled Frosting

- 1½ cups sugar
- ½ cup water
- 3 large egg whites, at room temperature
  Pinch of salt
- 1 teaspoon vanilla extract

Preheat the oven to 375 degrees. Grease and lightly flour two 9-inch round cake pans. Set aside.

Sift together the flour, baking powder and soda, cloves, cinnamon, nutmeg, and salt. Set aside. Cream the sugar and butter until fluffy, about 3 minutes. Beat in eggs 1 at a time, beating well after each addition. Stir in vanilla. Mix in the flour mixture, alternating with the mashed bananas.

Pour the batter into the prepared cake pans and bake for 25 minutes, or until a cake tester comes out clean. Allow to cool.

To make the icing, combine the sugar and water in a heavy saucepan over high heat and boil until the syrup reaches the soft-ball stage (238 degrees). Beat the egg whites with salt until they form soft peaks. Pour hot syrup, very slowly, into the beaten egg whites, then beat constantly with an electric mixer until frosting stands in stiff peaks and is of spreading consistency. Stir in vanilla.

To assemble the cake, place 1 layer on a flat cake plate, and cover the top with thin slices of ripe bananas. Sprinkle generously with granulated sugar. Put the other layer on top and hold in place with toothpicks. Cover the top and sides with frosting.

Serves 12

Blueberry Buckle

The owner and driving force behind the stylish Wolfman-Gold stores in New York City, Peri Wolfman, starting making blueberry buckle for her family when she lived in California years ago. Now that she has moved back east, she's planting blueberry bushes at her farm in Connecticut so she can get down to some serious blueberry buckling here.

 2 cups plus 1 to 2 tablespoons sifted all-purpose flour
 2 teaspoons baking powder
 ½ teaspoon salt
 ¼ cup (½ stick) unsalted butter, softened
 ¾ cup sugar
 1 large egg
 ½ cup milk
 1 pint blueberries
   Whipped cream flavored with rum

Topping
 ¼ cup (½ stick) unsalted butter, softened
 ½ cup sugar
 ⅓ cup sifted all-purpose flour
 ½ teaspoon ground cinnamon

Preheat the oven to 375 degrees. Grease an 8-inch springform pan. Set aside.

Sift together the 2 cups flour, baking powder, and salt. Set aside. Cream the butter and sugar until fluffy, about 3 minutes. Beat in the egg. Add the flour mixture in 3 parts, alternating with the milk. Toss the berries with the remaining tablespoon or 2 of flour (to separate and scatter evenly throughout the batter) and fold in. Pour batter into the prepared pan. Set aside.

Combine ingredients for topping with a fork to make a crumbly mixture. Sprinkle this over the batter, spreading it with your hand if you like.

Bake for 1 hour, then test for doneness by inserting a cake tester. If it does not come out clean, give the cake another 5 to 10 minutes to bake.

When the cake has cooled, run a knife around the edges and lift out of pan. Serve it with whipped cream generously spiked with rum (on the removable bottom of the pan if you like).

Serves 6 to 8

Brown Sugar Glazed Cake

This marvelous-tasting cake is from the fabulous Edna Lewis, who created it from her memory of such delicious simple cakes served when she was a child.

Incidentally, if you have never seen Ms. Lewis's lovely cookbook, The Taste of Country Cooking, *look it up—you're in for a treat.*

 2 cups minus 2 tablespoons sifted all-purpose flour
 1 tablespoon baking powder
   Scant ¼ teaspoon salt
 ½ cup (1 stick) unsalted butter, softened
 1½ cups superfine sugar
 3 large eggs
 ⅔ cup milk
 1 tablespoon vanilla extract

Glaze
 1 cup firmly packed light brown sugar
 3 tablespoons cold water

Preheat the oven to 375 degrees. Butter and flour a Bundt pan. Set aside.

Sift the flour, baking powder, and salt together. Set aside.

Cream the butter and sugar until fluffy, about 3 minutes. Add the eggs, 1 at a time, beating after each addition. Add the dry mixture in 3 parts, alternating with the milk. Stir in the vanilla and pour batter into the prepared pan.

Bake on the center rack of the oven for 35 minutes, or until a cake tester comes out clean.

Loosen the sides of the cake with a thin knife and allow cake to cool in the pan for about 15 minutes before removing to a rack to cool completely.

To make the glaze, place brown sugar and water in a medium saucepan set over medium heat and let boil until it reaches the soft-ball stage (234 to 240 degrees on a candy thermometer). Do not stir at any time during the cooking, but skim foam off top if necessary. Remove to a bowl of ice water, and when glaze becomes thick enough to spread, place cake on a rack set atop a layer of wax paper. Smooth or pour the glaze over the cake, letting it drip down the sides. If the glaze thickens too much, return to the pan and reheat to pouring consistency.

Serves 8 to 10

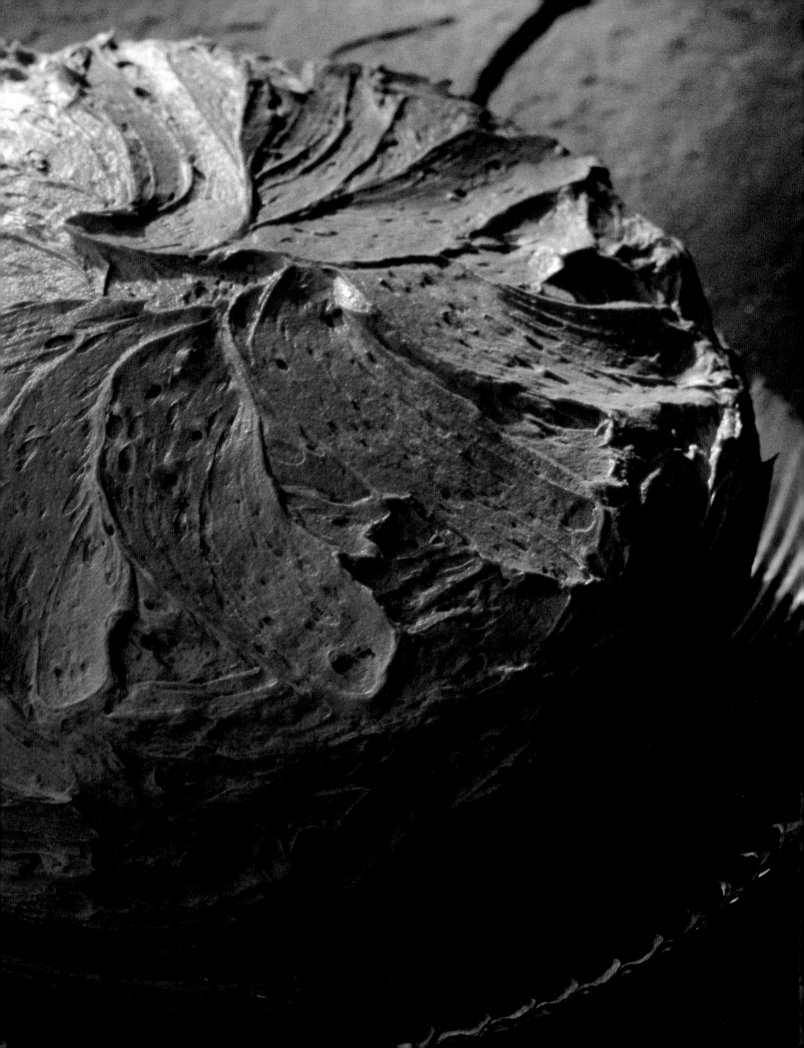

Opposite:
Devil's Food Cake with
Chocolate Buttercream Icing
Right: Chocolate Angel
Food Cake

Above: Coconut Cake
Left: Chocolate
Mousse Cheesecake

Chocolate Angel Food Cake

I've always been rather lukewarm about angel food cakes, but several years ago I got the idea to make a chocolate one and top it with Irish coffee sauce. I loved the way it came out, and it is easy to make.

   ¾ cup sifted cake flour (not self-rising)
   4 generous tablespoons good-quality
      unsweetened cocoa powder
1¼ cups large egg whites, at room temperature
      (from about 12 eggs)
   ¼ teaspoon salt
   1 teaspoon cream of tartar
1¼ cups sifted sugar
   1 teaspoon vanilla extract or lemon juice
      Irish Coffee Sauce (page 151)
   1 cup heavy cream, whipped
      Powdered instant espresso

Put rack in the center of the oven and preheat the oven to 375 degrees.

Tear off 2 large squares of wax paper and put the flour and cocoa together in a sifter and sift onto 1 of the squares. Repeat this process, going back and forth between the squares, until the flour and cocoa are well mixed—4 or 5 times. Set aside.

Beat the egg whites and salt until foamy, then sprinkle with cream of tartar. Continue beating until whites are stiff. Fold in the sugar a little at a time, using an over-and-under motion (always going in the same direction). Fold in vanilla, then the flour-cocoa mixture, using the same motion. Do not beat, but do this folding as quickly as possible.

Pour the batter into an ungreased 10-inch tube pan and bake for 30 minutes, or until cake tester comes out clean. Let cake cool completely before removing from the pan.

To serve, put a slick of coffee sauce on each dessert plate and on top of the sauce, place a slice of cake (cut the cake with a bread knife). Finish off by spooning some whipped cream over the top and sprinkling with a little powdered coffee.

Serves 12

Chocolate Mousse Cheesecake

Lynn Grossman, who gave me this recipe, is my kind of cook: She never leaves a recipe alone. For instance, sometimes her chocolate cheesecake has chocolate chips in it, and once she even put in broken pieces of chocolate Oreo cookies. (And she is thinking of adding chunks of white chocolate at this writing.)

Then sometimes, the crust is made with chocolate cookie crumbs instead of graham cracker crumbs, or a mixture of chocolate and graham cracker. There have also been times when you can't tell what the crust is made from. And often it is flavored with vanilla, but sometimes you will get a hint of almond or rum.

Well, you get the drift.

Crust
   ¾ cup graham cracker crumbs
   ¼ cup (½ stick) unsalted butter, softened
   2 tablespoons sugar

Filling
24 ounces cream cheese
   2 large eggs
   1 cup sugar
   8 ounces semisweet chocolate, melted
   2 tablespoons heavy cream
   7 tablespoons very strong coffee (espresso)
   ¾ cup sour cream
   1 teaspoon dark rum

Preheat the oven to 350 degrees.

To make the crust, place cracker crumbs, butter, and sugar in a food processor and give it a few whirls to mix. Press into the bottom of an 8-inch springform mold. Set aside.

To make the filling, put the cream cheese, eggs, and sugar into the processor bowl and mix until smooth. Add the remaining ingredients and blend thoroughly. Pour batter on top of the crust.

Bake for 45 minutes without opening the oven door (make sure your oven temperature is accurate). Cake will be slightly soft in the middle, but will firm up as it cools. At the end of the baking time, turn off heat and prop oven door open slightly with a pot holder or knife. Allow cake to cool in the oven for 1 hour before removing. Refrigerate.

Remove cake from the refrigerator at least 15 minutes before serving.

Serves 8 to 10

Coconut Cake

Mrs. Curtis McCaskill of Laurel, Mississippi, who is noted thereabouts for her wonderful desserts, told me how to make this cake. The recipe yields a very large cake that has a marvelous "old-fashioned" flavor and is delicious served with fruit. It also keeps quite well. As a matter of fact, Mrs. McCaskill likes this cake better the second or third day. I tried it after two days, and she may be right.

- 3 cups sifted all-purpose flour
- ¼ teaspoon baking soda
- 1 cup (2 sticks) unsalted butter, softened
- 3 cups sugar
- 6 large eggs
- 8 ounces sour cream
- 1 tablespoon coconut flavoring
- ½ teaspoon vanilla extract
  Boiled Frosting (page 26) or White Mountain Icing (page 42)
  Grated fresh coconut

Preheat the oven to 350 degrees. Grease and lightly flour a 10-inch tube pan.

Sift the flour and baking soda, then set aside.

Cream the butter and sugar until fluffy, about 3 minutes. Then add eggs 1 at a time, beating well after each addition. Add dry mixture, alternating with the sour cream. Stir in the flavorings and pour into the prepared pan. Bake for approximately 70 minutes (or slightly more), or until a cake tester comes out clean. Allow cake to cool completely before removing from the pan.

Ice the cake, then sprinkle it generously with freshly grated coconut.

Serves 12 to 18

Devil's Food Cake with Chocolate Buttercream Icing

Although a chocolate frosting is the classic for devil's food, some people prefer other frostings (vanilla or coffee) for a contrast in color and flavor. I generally like classics the way they are, especially this one.

- 1⅔ cups sifted cake flour (not self-rising)
- ¼ cup unsweetened cocoa powder
- 1 teaspoon baking soda
- ½ teaspoon salt
- ½ cup (1 stick) unsalted butter, softened
- 1½ cups firmly packed dark brown sugar
- 1½ teaspoons vanilla extract
- 2 large eggs
- 2 ounces unsweetened chocolate, melted and cooled
- ¾ cup strong hot coffee (not instant)

Chocolate Buttercream Icing
- 1 cup (2 sticks) unsalted butter, softened
- 1 large egg yolk, at room temperature
- 6 ounces semisweet chocolate, melted and cooled
- 1 tablespoon powdered instant espresso
- 1 teaspoon vanilla extract
- 1¼ cups sifted confectioners' sugar

Preheat the oven to 350 degrees. Grease and flour two 9-inch round cake pans.

Sift together the flour, cocoa, baking soda, and salt. Set aside.

Cream the butter and brown sugar until smooth, about 3 minutes, then stir in the vanilla. Add the eggs, 1 at a time, beating 2 minutes after each addition. Beat in the melted chocolate and gradually stir in the hot coffee.

Add the flour mixture, one third at the time, beating well after each addition. Pour batter into the prepared pans and bake for 25 minutes, or until a cake tester comes out clean.

Let the layers cool in the pan for 10 minutes. Unmold onto cake racks and let cool completely.

To make icing, cream the butter until fluffy, about 3 minutes. Beat in the egg yolk, then add the melted chocolate and beat well. Add the espresso and vanilla and beat for 3 minutes. Gradually add the confectioners' sugar and beat, scraping bowl as necessary, until smooth and creamy.

When cake has cooled, ice between the layers, then ice top and sides of cake.

Serves 8 to 12

Left to right:
Sunshine Cream Cake;
Plantation Pecan Cake;
Marble Cake

Plantation Pecan Cake

In New Orleans, Margaret Williams used to serve this cake, which is popular wherever pecans are grown. Sometimes the cake was cooked in a tube pan and at other times in layers, as it is here. Whichever way, it has always been one of my favorites.

1½ cups sifted all-purpose flour
1 teaspoon baking powder
½ teaspoon salt
1½ cups finely chopped or grated pecans
½ cup (1 stick) unsalted butter, softened
1½ cups sugar
¼ cup bourbon mixed with ½ cup water
½ cup egg whites, stiffly beaten (from about 5 medium eggs)
1 cup heavy cream, whipped
Confectioners' sugar

Preheat the oven to 375 degrees. Grease two 8-inch round cake pans and cut wax paper to fit the bottom of each. Grease the papers and then lightly flour the inside of each pan. Set aside.

Sift together the flour, baking powder, and salt. Combine with pecans and set aside.

Cream the butter and sugar until fluffy, about 3 minutes. Add the dry mixture in 4 parts, alternating with the bourbon water and mixing well after each addition. Pile the beaten egg whites on top of the batter and carefully fold in with an over-and-under motion.

Pour batter into pans and bake for approximately 25 minutes, or until a cake tester comes out clean. Allow layers to cool for about 10 minutes, then run a knife around the edges of the pans and invert onto cooling racks.

To serve cake, place whipped cream between the 2 layers, holding them in place with a couple of toothpicks if necessary. Sift confectioners' sugar over the top.

Serves 12

Sunshine Cream Cake

Another all-time winner, this version of the classic is served at Watts Tea Room in Milwaukee, Wisconsin.

9 large eggs, separated, at room temperature
¼ cup water
1½ teaspoons vanilla
1½ teaspoons ground cinnamon
1 cup granulated sugar
1 cup cake flour (not self-rising), sifted 3 times
1 teaspoon cream of tartar
¼ teaspoon salt

French Custard Filling
4 large egg yolks, lightly beaten
¾ cup sifted confectioners' sugar
¾ cup milk
1 teaspoon vanilla extract
1 cup (2 sticks) unsalted butter

Boiled Frosting (page 26)

Garnish
Grated orange peel

Preheat the oven to 350 degrees.

Combine the egg yolks, water, vanilla, cinnamon, and ½ cup sugar in a large bowl. Beat together until light and fluffy. Add flour, ¼ cup at a time, until well blended.

Whip egg whites with cream of tartar until they form soft peaks. Add remaining ½ cup sugar and beat until stiff peaks begin to form. Fold whites into batter. Pour into an ungreased 9-inch tube pan and bake for 35 minutes. Let cool thoroughly in pan for about 15 minutes, then remove from pan to rack to finish cooling.

To make filling, combine egg yolks, confectioners' sugar, and milk in the top of a double boiler, and cook, stirring constantly, until custard coats a stirring spoon and begins to thicken. Let cool.

Combine vanilla and butter in a bowl and cream until fluffy, about 2 minutes. Add custard slowly and continue beating mixture until smooth.

To assemble, cut cake carefully into 3 layers. Spread custard filling between the layers, then ice top and sides with frosting. Garnish with grated orange peel.

Serves 12

Marble Cake

This cake calls for both white and chocolate icing, but if you don't want to put white icing between the layers, then use chocolate icing for all of it. However, we thought as long as we are making this classic mixed-up cake, we might as well go all the way and mix up the icing, too.

  1 ounce unsweetened chocolate, melted
  1 teaspoon powdered instant espresso
  1 teaspoon ground cinnamon
2¼ cups sifted cake flour (not self-rising)
  1 tablespoon baking powder
  1 teaspoon baking soda
  ¼ teaspoon salt
  ½ cup (1 stick) unsalted butter, softened
1¼ cups granulated sugar
  2 large eggs
  ¾ cup sour cream
1½ teaspoons vanilla extract
  6 tablespoons milk

Icing
  ½ cup (1 stick) unsalted butter, softened
  1 teaspoon vanilla extract
3½ cups (1 box) confectioners' sugar, sifted
  ¼ cup milk
1½ teaspoons ground cinnamon
  2 ounces unsweetened chocolate, melted
    and cooled

Preheat the oven to 350 degrees. Butter and flour two 9-inch round cake pans. Set aside.

Combine the melted chocolate with the powdered espresso and the cinnamon. Set aside to cool.

Sift together the flour, baking powder, baking soda, and salt. Set aside.

Cream the butter and sugar until fluffy, about 3 minutes. Add the eggs, 1 at a time, beating well after each addition. Add the sour cream and vanilla, then mix well. Add the dry mixture in 3 batches, alternating with the milk. Combine well.

Divide batter in half and stir the chocolate mixture into one half. Pour half the white batter into each cake pan, spooning it onto one side of the pan. Divide the chocolate batter between the two pans and, using the blade of a table knife, swirl the white and chocolate batters together to marbleize them. Tap pans on a hard surface to settle the batters.

Bake the layers on 2 oven racks, reversing their positions after 15 minutes. Bake 10 to 15 minutes more, or until a cake tester comes out clean. Let layers cool slightly in the pan before turning out onto racks to cool completely.

To make icing, cream the butter until light and fluffy, about 2 minutes, then beat in vanilla. Gradually add the confectioners' sugar, alternating with the milk, until icing is thick and smooth. Beat in ½ teaspoon of the cinnamon.

Place the bottom cake layer on a cake plate and ice its top only; do not ice sides. Place the second layer on top, holding it in place with toothpicks if necessary. Stir the melted chocolate and remaining cinnamon into the icing and mix well. Ice the top and sides of the cake with the chocolate icing.

Serves 8 to 12

Above: Flourless Chocolate Cake
Below: Fresh Pineapple Upside-Down Cake
Right: Fresh Peach Cake

Flourless Chocolate Cake

Well, this may not be "death by chocolate," but it is close to being an overdose. Chocolate freaks will love it! Serve this in small wedges; this stuff is intense. And complement it with a dab of whipped cream.

> 5 ounces bittersweet or semisweet chocolate
> 3 ounces unsweetened chocolate
> ½ cup (1 stick) unsalted butter, softened
> 5 large eggs, separated, at room temperature
> ⅔ cup sugar
> 1½ teaspoons vanilla extract
>   Pinch of salt
>
> ### Glaze
> 3 ounces semisweet chocolate
> 3 tablespoons unsalted butter, softened
> 1 tablespoon brandy or bourbon (optional, but I think necessary)

Preheat the oven to 350 degrees. Butter and flour a 10-inch springform pan. Line the bottom with a round of parchment or wax paper, then butter the paper. Set aside.

For the cake, melt the chocolates and butter together in a saucepan set over low heat, stirring to blend well. Set aside to cool.

Beat the egg yolks with the sugar until thick and lemon yellow in color, about 5 minutes. Stir in the vanilla.

Whisk the egg whites with the salt until stiff. Set aside.

Gently fold the chocolate mixture into the yolks, then fold in one third of the egg whites. Fold in remaining whites until no streaks of white remain.

Pour batter into the prepared pan and bake in the center of the oven for 35 to 45 minutes, or until a cake tester inserted in the center comes out clean. The cake will rise a great deal during baking.

Cool cake in pan for 10 minutes, then remove sides of the pan. Invert the cake onto a rack and remove the bottom, but do not remove the parchment. Let cake cool completely; it will fall considerably. Remove parchment before glazing.

To make glaze, melt the chocolate and butter together in a saucepan over low heat, stirring until smooth. Stir in the brandy.

Place the cake on a rack set over a sheet of wax paper. Pour glaze over cake and spread lightly with a spatula, if necessary, to coat cake evenly, allowing extra glaze to run down sides.

Serves 10 to 12

Fresh Peach Cake

I'm told this is an old Pennsylvania Dutch recipe, but I wouldn't swear to it. Wherever it came from, it's hard to resist.

> 2 cups sifted all-purpose flour
> 5 tablespoons plus 1 teaspoon cornstarch
> 2 teaspoons baking powder
> ¾ teaspoon salt
> 6 tablespoons (¾ stick) margarine, softened
> 6 tablespoons (¾ stick) unsalted butter, softened
> 1¼ cups plus 2 tablespoons sugar
> ¾ cup milk
> 1½ teaspoons vanilla extract
> 9 large egg whites, stiffly beaten
>
> ### Cream Filling
> 2 cups heavy cream
> ½ cup sugar
> 1½ teaspoons vanilla extract
>
> ### Peach Filling
> 5 to 6 large peaches
>   Juice of ½ lemon
> 2 tablespoons sugar

Make cream filling first. Mix cream, sugar, and vanilla. Cover and refrigerate for at least 2 hours.

Preheat the oven to 350 degrees. Generously grease three 8-inch round cake pans, then line the bottoms with wax paper. Grease the paper and lightly flour. Set aside.

Sift the flour with the cornstarch, baking powder, and salt. Set aside.

Cream the margarine, butter, and sugar until fluffy, about 3 minutes. Add the dry mixture in 4 parts, alternating with the milk and ending with the flour. Mix in the vanilla.

Place the beaten egg whites on top of the mixture and fold in with an over-and-under motion. Do not beat, but be sure it is well mixed. Pour batter into cake pans and bake on the middle rack of the oven for 20 to 25 minutes, or until a cake tester comes out clean. Let cakes cool in pans for 10 minutes, then invert onto cooling racks. Let cool completely.

To assemble cake, dip peaches in hot water for about 10 seconds, then run cold water over them. Slip the skins off and cut each into about a dozen slices; discard pits. Toss peach slices with the lemon juice and sugar. Whip the chilled cream-sugar filling until it is stiff, then mix in the vanilla.

The peaches will have given up a bit of juice by

now, so pour some of it over the bottom cake layer, a little at a time, to give it a chance to soak in. Put a third of the peach slices on this bottom layer and cover with some whipped cream. Repeat with the remaining layers, holding them in place with toothpicks if necessary.

Keep cake refrigerated, very loosely covered with foil or wax paper, until ready to serve.

Serves 12 to 18

Fresh Pineapple Upside-Down Cake

Once you taste this light version of the classic pineapple cake, you will never use canned pineapple again.

Pineapple Bottom Layer
¼ cup (½ stick) unsalted butter
½ cup firmly packed dark brown sugar
2 tablespoons dark rum
1 ripe pineapple, peeled, cored, and cut into at least 8 rings
8 to 12 pecan halves

Cake Layer
2 cups sifted cake flour (not self-rising)
2 teaspoons baking powder
¼ teaspoon salt
½ cup (1 stick) unsalted butter, softened
1 cup granulated sugar
2 large eggs
2 teaspoons vanilla extract
1 cup pineapple juice (canned or fresh)

Preheat the oven to 350 degrees.

To prepare the pineapple bottom, place the butter, brown sugar, and rum in an 11-inch cast-iron skillet and put it in the oven until the butter and sugar melt, about 7 to 10 minutes. Mix well.

Arrange the pineapple rings over the bottom of the skillet, cutting some in half, if necessary, to cover the surface. Put the pecan halves, rounded side down, in the center of each ring. Set aside.

To make the cake layer, sift together the flour, baking powder, and salt. Set aside.

Cream the butter and sugar until fluffy, about 3 minutes. Add the dry mixture a little at a time, beating until well incorporated. Add the eggs, 1 at a time, beating well after each addition. Add the vanilla and the pineapple juice and beat well. Pour the batter over the pineapple layer and smooth the top.

Bake for 40 to 45 minutes, or until deep golden brown and a toothpick inserted in the center comes out clean. Cool cake on a rack, then turn out onto a serving plate.

Serves 8 to 12

German Chocolate Cake

Here is a darker, richer version of the familiar cake, done up with a crunchy coconut-pecan icing. This is shown in the picture on page 21.

2¼ cups sifted cake flour (not self-rising)
1 teaspoon baking soda
½ teaspoon salt
½ cup (1 stick) unsalted butter, softened
1 cup firmly packed dark brown sugar
5 large eggs
1 teaspoon vanilla extract
7 ounces milk chocolate, grated
1 cup buttermilk

Coconut-Pecan Icing
1 cup (8 ounces) evaporated milk
2 tablespoons (¼ stick) unsalted butter
⅔ cup firmly packed dark brown sugar
2 large egg yolks
1 teaspoon vanilla extract
¾ cup chopped pecans
1½ cups shredded fresh coconut

Preheat the oven to 350 degrees. Butter two 8-inch square baking pans and dust them with cocoa powder. Set aside.

Sift together the flour, baking soda, and salt. Set aside.

Cream the butter and sugar until smooth, about 3 minutes. Add the eggs, 1 at the time, beating about 1 minute after each addition. Stir in the vanilla and the chocolate.

Add the dry mixture in thirds, alternating with the buttermilk. Beat until smooth, then pour batter into prepared pans.

Bake for 35 to 40 minutes, or until a cake tester comes out clean. Cool cake in the pans for 10 minutes, then unmold onto cake racks to cool to room temperature.

To make icing, combine evaporated milk, butter, brown sugar, and egg yolks in a large saucepan and stir over moderate heat. Continue to cook, stirring constantly, for 12 minutes or until very thick.

Stir in the vanilla off the heat, then add the pecans and coconut. Stir to moisten well. Spread the icing between the layers first, then ice the top.

Serves 10 to 12

Above: Intermont White Cake. *Below:* Golden Pecan Cake with Pecan Divinity Icing. *Opposite:* Lane Cake

Golden Pecan Cake with Pecan Divinity Icing

This is one of everyone's favorites. It should be served with ice cream, whipped cream, or vanilla sauce.

 3 cups sifted all-purpose flour (not self-rising)
 1½ teaspoons baking powder
 ¼ teaspoon salt
 1 cup coarsely chopped toasted pecans
 1 cup (2 sticks) unsalted butter, softened
 2 cups sugar
 5 large eggs
 1 cup milk
 1 teaspoon vanilla extract

Pecan Divinity Icing

 3 cups sugar
 ½ cup light corn syrup
 ⅔ cup water
 2 large egg whites, at room temperature
  Pinch of salt
 1 teaspoon vanilla extract
 1 cup chopped toasted pecans *

Preheat the oven to 350 degrees. Oil and lightly flour three 9-inch round cake pans. Set aside.

Sift together the flour, baking powder, and salt. Remove ¼ cup of the mixture and toss with the pecans. Set both aside.

Cream the butter and sugar until light and fluffy, about 3 minutes. Add eggs, 1 at a time, mixing well after each addition. Add the dry ingredients in 3 batches, alternating with the milk and mixing well after each addition. Add the vanilla and mix, then fold in the floured pecans. (Do not overmix.)

Pour batter into prepared pans and bake for 30 minutes, or until tops are golden and sides have left the pan. Remove and allow to cool slightly before inverting onto cooling racks. Let cool completely.

To make icing, combine sugar, syrup, and water in a large saucepan. Bring to a boil over medium heat and continue to boil until mixture reaches soft-ball stage (238 degrees on a candy thermometer).

Meanwhile, beat the egg whites with the salt until stiff. When syrup is ready, pour into the beaten egg whites in a thin, steady stream, beating all the while. When creamy, stir in the vanilla.

Ice the cake by filling between layers first and sprinkling with pecans, then ice the top and sides and sprinkle top with remaining nuts.

Serves approximately 12

* Chopped candied cherries and freshly grated coconut can also be sprinkled between the layers and on top, along with the pecans.

Intermont White Cake

My Aunt Cora used to make this cake for celebrations. It has a marvelous light texture and looks beautiful piled generously with white mountain icing. This is scrumptious with peach pit ice cream or homemade vanilla-bean (pages 10 and 18).

 3 cups sifted cake flour (not self-rising)
 1 tablespoon baking powder
 ½ teaspoon salt
 ¾ cup (1½ sticks) unsalted butter, softened
 2 cups sugar
 1 teaspoon vanilla extract
 1 teaspoon almond extract
 1 cup milk
 6 large egg whites, at room temperature

White Mountain Icing

 1 cup boiling water
 2¼ cups sugar
 1 tablespoon light corn syrup
 3 large egg whites, at room temperature
 1 teaspoon vanilla extract

Preheat the oven to 375 degrees. Grease and lightly flour two 9-inch round cake pans. Set aside.

Sift together the flour, baking powder, and salt. Set aside. Cream the butter and 1½ cups of the sugar until fluffy, about 3 minutes. Mix in the vanilla and almond extracts. Add the dry mixture in 4 parts, alternating with the milk.

Whisk the egg whites until foamy, then start adding the remaining ½ cup sugar, continuing to beat until whites stand in stiff peaks. Fold whites into the batter with an over-and-under motion. Pour batter into the prepared pans and bake for 35 minutes, or until a cake tester comes out clean. Allow to cool slightly, then loosen edges and remove from the pans to cake racks to cool completely.

To make the icing, combine the boiling water with 2 cups of the sugar and the corn syrup in a large saucepan set over medium heat. Cook at a rolling boil until mixture reaches soft-ball stage (238 degrees on a candy thermometer).

Meanwhile, whisk whites until foamy, then start adding the remaining ¼ cup sugar. Continue whisking until whites stand in stiff peaks.

When syrup is at the correct temperature, pour into the beaten whites in a thin, steady stream, beating all the while. Ice between the cake layers, then ice the top and sides of the cake.

Serves 12 to 18

Lane Cake

Lane cake is a relative of the Lord Baltimore cake and other variations on the theme of light, thin-layered cakes filled with nuts, candied fruit, and coconut. They are rich and perfect for a special occasion. This version came from my friend Sherrye Henry.

3¼ cups sifted all-purpose flour
1 tablespoon plus ½ teaspoon baking powder
½ teaspoon salt
1 cup (2 sticks) unsalted butter, softened
2 cups sugar
1 teaspoon vanilla extract
1 cup milk
8 large egg whites, stiffly beaten

Filling
8 large egg yolks, at room temperature
1¾ cups sugar
½ cup (1 stick) unsalted butter, softened
1 cup coarsely chopped pecans
1 cup freshly grated coconut, or 1 can (3½ ounces) sweetened grated coconut
1 cup coarsely chopped candied cherries
1 cup finely chopped raisins
6 tablespoons bourbon

Icing
1¼ cups plus 2 tablespoons dark corn syrup
2 large egg whites, stiffly beaten with a pinch of salt
1 teaspoon vanilla extract

Preheat the oven to 375 degrees. Cut circles of wax paper to fit the bottoms of 4 greased 9-inch round cake pans. Grease papers, then set pans aside.

Sift together the flour, baking powder, and salt. Set aside. Cream the butter and sugar until fluffy, about 3 minutes. Mix in the vanilla. Add dry mixture in 4 parts, alternating with the milk and mixing well after each addition. Carefully fold in the beaten egg whites with an over-and-under motion.

Pour batter in equal portions into the prepared pans. Bake for 15 minutes (or slightly more), until

cake tester comes out clean. Allow layers to cool in pans while you make the filling.

To make filling, beat yolks with the sugar until a light yellow color. Beat in the softened butter until well combined. Transfer to a large saucepan set over low heat and cook until mixture starts to thicken, stirring all the while, about 5 minutes. Add the pecans, coconut, cherries, raisins, and bourbon. Mix thoroughly and allow to cool.

Assemble the cake. Run a knife around the edges of the cake pans and invert layers onto cooling racks. Tap and shake pans until layers come out, then remove the wax paper. Fill between the layers with the fruit and nut mixture, distributing it evenly.

To make icing, bring syrup to a rolling boil in a small saucepan over medium heat, then immediately pour it, in a thin, steady stream, into the beaten egg whites. Continue to beat until icing cools and thickens. Stir in vanilla. Pour out onto the top of the cake and coax down the sides. Spread icing on sides with a rubber spatula.

Serves 18 to 24

Coffee and Tea

Coffee and Tea

T ea or coffee in the afternoon with a little sweet is the best of all pauses. For it is about five o'clock when most of us start to run out of steam and are in need of a pick-me-up. It's especially true in my case, because I like to have a very late dinner, and afternoon tea helps bridge the gap. Although mid-morning coffee was very popular where I grew up (as well as afternoon coffee), I never got the habit. Be that as it may, the sweets that follow are perfect accompaniments to good strong coffee and tea (either hot or iced), mornings or afternoons. And some, like the applesauce cake and the gingerbread, can double as desserts. Others, such as the Bishop's bread and the cinnamon-oatmeal raisin bread, are fine for breakfast.

As usually happens when I sit down to write about food, the recipes start to remind me of other things, until finally I get back to my childhood where most of my best food memories were formed. There is a particular Christmas cake, a white fruitcake, I remember. Although it is delicious, it isn't so much the cake's flavor that sticks in my memory as the pedigree by which it was always accompanied. I had actually forgotten this bit of foolishness until I came across the recipe, folded up in my grandmother's cookbook.

You see, the recipe belonged to a rather fancy friend of my grandmother's, and whenever her friend served it you would be told (as if you hadn't heard it before), while the cake was being passed around, that this very self-same white fruitcake you were about to eat was a great favorite of the Duchess of Windsor. Undoubtedly, the friend felt this bit of "inside" knowledge would somehow make the occasion—and the cake, I suppose—more august. In truth, it is probably near to impossible to make a cake august.

Well, this white fruitcake may well have been the duchess's favorite, for all any of us knew, but I always wondered *how* my grandmother's friend knew it to be. You see, the D. of W. never visited Bunkie, Louisiana (where this all took place), or I would surely have heard about it. Even if there had been such social high jinks going on, you just can't keep news like that secret in a town of 3,000 people. And while I suppose the fancy lady and the duchess *could* have met in New Orleans or Gulfport occasionally to exchange recipes (she had been just over in the Bahamas then, after all), I probably would have heard about that, too.

Alas, I guess we are doomed never to know the truth of it, since both of them are gone now—eating white fruitcake together on some tasteful cloud, no doubt, between sets on the harp.

Many of the cakes in this chapter seem to improve with a few days' age—which is fine, because you certainly seldom finish a cake at a single sitting unless you have a large group of guests. And some, like the nut and fruitcakes, can go on indefinitely if carefully wrapped and stored in airtight containers. Many fruitcakes get doused regularly with whiskey or brandy. While I like the taste of both in food, I'm not too fond of cakes preserved in this manner, since the liquor quickly becomes overpowering.

When you do find yourself with stale cake, the drier ones can be used to make crumb pie crusts or incorporated into triflelike concoctions. So don't throw anything out before considering all the possibilities.

One of my favorite afternoon snacks is slightly stale pound cake that is buttered and toasted under the broiler. Sometimes I think it is even better that way than when fresh.

Stale cake can also be cut into large cubes and stirred into a custard, then baked, making a delicious dessert when topped with a spiked whipped cream (page 150).

Another use for stale cake crumbs is as a topping for custard or ice cream. Simply crumble the cake and toast or dry the crumbs in a very low oven (250 degrees). You could also add coarsely chopped toasted nuts.

Finally, if you are going to serve a special cake, don't destroy the whole effort by serving inferior coffee or tea. There are so many kinds to choose from; do a little testing and experimenting if you haven't already done so, until you find something that suits your palate. I often combine an espresso with another kind to make my own blend. You might do the same.

I think the aromatic teas and spiced coffees are not appropriate here, because the very spices and herbs added to them can compete with the flavor of the cakes. You want a good and strong flavor with a rich and unadorned taste that will enhance the flavor of your cake. Ideally, the milk or cream served with it should be heated.

And never, never serve instant tea or coffee on such occasions. I'm sure you already know that, but I'm just reminding you.

COFFEE AND TEA 47

Left: Apple-Cinnamon,
Banana-Walnut, and Blueberry Muffins
Above: Applesauce-Spice Cake
Below: Bishop's Bread

Apple-Cinnamon Muffins

Like the other muffins that follow, these are perfect to serve in the afternoon or for breakfast.

> 2 cups sifted all-purpose flour
> 1 tablespoon baking powder
> 1½ teaspoons ground cinnamon
> 1 teaspoon salt
> 3 large eggs
> ⅔ cup milk
> 6 tablespoons (¾ stick) unsalted butter, melted
> ½ teaspoon vanilla extract
> ½ cup firmly packed light brown sugar
> 1 cup peeled, seeded, and chopped apple

Preheat the oven to 400 degrees. Grease 12 muffin cups. Set aside.

Sift together the flour, baking powder, cinnamon, and salt. Set aside. Combine the eggs, milk, butter, and vanilla in a bowl and mix well. Beat in the brown sugar, then add the flour. Stir in the apple, but do not overmix; batter should be lumpy. Divide batter among the cups.

Bake for 20 to 25 minutes, or just until a cake tester comes out clean.

Makes 1 dozen

Banana-Walnut Muffins

If you prefer, bake these (and others) in pleated paper cups, which are placed in muffin tins. Obviously, they make muffins easier to remove from the tin and there is less washing up later.

> 2 cups sifted all-purpose flour
> 1 tablespoon baking powder
> 1 teaspoon salt
> 3 large eggs
> ⅔ cup milk
> 6 tablespoons (¾ stick) unsalted butter, melted
> ½ cup firmly packed dark brown sugar
> ½ teaspoon vanilla extract
> 1½ cups mashed banana (2 to 3 ripe bananas)
> ⅓ cup chopped walnuts

Preheat the oven to 400 degrees. Grease 12 muffin cups. Set aside.

Sift together the flour, baking powder, and salt. Set aside. Combine the eggs, milk, and melted butter in a bowl. Mix well, then beat in the brown sugar and vanilla. Add the dry ingredients and mix slightly. Stir in the bananas and nuts. Combine but do not overmix; the batter should be lumpy. Divide among the cups.

Bake for 20 to 25 minutes, or until a cake tester comes out clean.

Makes 1 dozen

Blueberry Muffins

This recipe calls for lots of berries, which is the way I like these muffins.

> 2 cups plus 3 tablespoons sifted all-purpose flour
> ½ teaspoon salt
> 4 teaspoons baking powder
> ½ teaspoon ground cinnamon
> ½ cup plus 2 tablespoons sugar
> 2 large eggs, well beaten
> 6 tablespoons (¾ stick) unsalted butter, melted
> ⅔ cup milk
> 2½ cups blueberries

Preheat the oven to 425 degrees. Either grease a 12- and a 6-cup muffin tin or place 16 paper cups in the muffin tins. Set aside.

Sift together 2 cups of the flour, salt, baking powder, and cinnamon. Set aside.

Beat together the sugar and eggs, then add the melted butter and milk, mixing well. Briefly stir in the dry mixture, being careful not to overmix. Sprinkle the remaining flour over the blueberries to coat them, then fold into the batter.

Fill the muffin cups about two thirds full.

Bake for 20 to 25 minutes, or until a cake tester comes out clean.

Makes 16

Applesauce-Spice Cake

This is one of my all-time favorite cakes. It remains moist and fresh for a long time, especially if stored in an airtight container. As a matter of fact, its flavor seems to improve the second day.

It can be served for dessert with the addition of a flavored cream or a sauce. But how this cake really shines is with coffee or tea.

Incidentally, the brown sugar frosting does double duty as a candy, by simply adding ½ cup or so of chopped nuts and pouring the mixture out onto a buttered shallow plate to cool. Cut into squares and serve.

  1 cup (2 sticks) unsalted butter, softened
  2 cups superfine sugar
  2 cups good-quality unsweetened applesauce
  3 cups sifted all-purpose flour
  1 cup coarsely chopped pecans
  1 cup raisins
  1 teaspoon ground cinnamon
  1 teaspoon grated nutmeg
 ½ teaspoon mace
1¾ teaspoons baking soda
  1 teaspoon vanilla extract

Brown Sugar Frosting

  2 cups firmly packed light brown sugar
  6 tablespoons heavy cream
 ¼ cup (½ stick) unsalted butter
  1 teaspoon vanilla extract
  1 cup sifted confectioners' sugar

Preheat the oven to 325 degrees. Grease a 9-inch tube pan. Cut a piece of wax paper to fit the bottom and grease it lightly. Dust the pan with flour, shaking out excess.

Cream the butter and superfine sugar until fluffy, about 3 minutes. Then fold in the applesauce. This will not mix completely, but don't be alarmed.

Remove ¼ cup of the flour and use it to dredge the nuts and raisins. Sift together the remaining flour, spices, and baking soda. Fold the dry mixture into the creamed mixture, then add the vanilla and the nuts and raisins.

Pour batter into the prepared pan and bake for 1½ hours, or until a cake tester comes out clean. Allow cake to cool in the pan, then invert to remove.

Place all the ingredients for the frosting except the vanilla and the confectioners' sugar into a large saucepan and slowly bring to a rolling boil over medium heat, stirring all the while. Remove pan from heat and stir in the vanilla and then the confectioners' sugar. Pour frosting onto the top of the cake and let run down the sides. This frosting tends to set rather quickly, so don't try to spread it with a spatula; it will look best if allowed to flow naturally.

Serves 12 to 14

Bishop's Bread

Pam Lockard has triplets and another daughter, so she is pretty busy around the house. However, she says she has time to make this easy and tasty old "bread" from the recipe that follows. It's perfect, not only for tea or coffee, but in the morning, toasted.

2½ cups sifted all-purpose flour
  2 cups firmly packed light brown sugar
  1 teaspoon salt
 ½ cup solid vegetable shortening
  1 teaspoon baking powder
  1 teaspoon baking soda
  1 teaspoon ground cinnamon
 ¾ cup milk
  1 tablespoon distilled white vinegar
  1 large egg

Preheat the oven to 375 degrees. Grease a 9 x 13-inch baking pan. Set aside.

With a hand mixer, combine the flour, brown sugar, and salt in a large bowl. Cut in the shortening with a pastry blender or 2 knives until it resembles the texture of coarse meal. Set aside ¾ cup of this mixture in a small bowl to use later as the topping.

Add the baking powder, soda, and cinnamon to the large bowl and mix. Stir in the milk, vinegar, and egg and mix with a hand mixer at high speed until mixture is smooth.

Pour batter into the prepared pan and sprinkle the reserved crumb topping evenly over the top.

Bake for 25 minutes, or until golden. Allow to cool in the pan before cutting into approximately 3 x 2-inch squares. Serve warm or at room temperature.

Serves 18

Above: Golden Raisin Gingerbread. _Below:_ Carrot Cake with Cream Cheese Icing

Above: Cinnamon-Oatmeal Raisin Bread. _Below:_ Nut Cake

Carrot Cake with Cream Cheese Icing

What more can be said about carrot cake, which the "back to the earth" hippies of the '60s made famous. This version is moist and spicy—and terrific.

      2 cups sifted whole wheat flour
   1½ teaspoons baking soda
   1½ teaspoons ground cinnamon
   1½ teaspoons ground allspice
   1½ cups vegetable oil
      1 cup granulated sugar
      4 large eggs
      ½ cup buttermilk
      4 cups finely grated carrots (about 1¾ pounds)
      ½ cup chopped walnuts

   Cream Cheese Icing
      1 package (8 ounces) cream cheese, at room temperature
      ⅓ cup sour cream
      2 tablespoons (¼ stick) unsalted butter, softened
      1 cup sifted confectioners' sugar

Preheat the oven to 325 degrees. Grease a 9 x 13-inch glass baking pan. Set aside.

Sift together the flour, baking soda, cinnamon, and allspice. Set aside.

Beat together the oil and sugar until sugar is dissolved and mixture is smooth, about 3 minutes. Add the eggs, 1 at the time, mixing well after each addition. Gradually add the dry mixture, alternating with the buttermilk. Beat well.

Fold in the carrots and walnuts, combining well, then pour batter into prepared pan and smooth the top with a spatula.

Bake for 40 to 45 minutes, or until a cake tester comes out clean. Let cool on cake rack.

To make icing, cream the cream cheese, sour cream, and butter until fluffy. Add the confectioners' sugar and beat until thickened. Spread over room-temperature cake and refrigerate until served.

Serves 12

Cinnamon-Oatmeal Raisin Bread

Not too sweet, yet comforting, tasty, and spicy. Who could ask for anything more?

      1 scant cup rolled oats
      ¾ cup scalded milk
      1 scant cup golden raisins
   1½ cups sifted whole wheat flour
   1¼ cups sifted all-purpose flour
      1 tablespoon baking powder
      1 teaspoon baking soda
      1 teaspoon salt
      1 tablespoon ground cinnamon
      ½ teaspoon freshly grated nutmeg
      ¾ cup (1½ sticks) unsalted butter, softened
      1 cup firmly packed light brown sugar
      3 large eggs
      ½ cup sour cream
      2 teaspoons vanilla extract

Combine the oats, milk, and raisins in a bowl. Stir to moisten thoroughly, then set aside for 45 minutes to 1 hour.

Preheat the oven to 350 degrees. Butter and flour two 9 x 5 x 3-inch loaf pans.

Combine the flours, baking powder and soda, salt, and spices in a bowl. Set aside.

Cream the butter and brown sugar until smooth, about 3 minutes. Add eggs, 1 at a time, beating well after each addition. Beat in sour cream and vanilla, then add oatmeal-raisin mixture (all the milk will have been absorbed).

Lightly mix in the flour mixture, one third at the time. The dough should be thick, lumpy, and sticky. Divide batter between the 2 pans.

Bake loaves on the center rack of the oven for 35 to 40 minutes, or until a cake tester comes out *almost* clean. Do not overbake. Allow bread to cool in the pans for about 15 minutes, then unmold onto racks. When completely cooled, wrap in foil and keep at room temperature for a few days or freeze. The flavor improves with age.

Makes 2 loaves

Golden Raisin Gingerbread

This gingerbread is marvelous with tea or coffee. But it can also be served warm with ice cream or bourbon whipped cream (page 150) as a dessert.

Most gingerbread recipes are pretty much the same, but this one calls for light raisins, which I like best, instead of the usual dark ones. If you don't like raisins, leave them out altogether.

2¼ cups sifted all-purpose flour
1 teaspoon baking soda
1 teaspoon baking powder
½ teaspoon salt
1 tablespoon ground ginger
½ teaspoon ground cinnamon
½ cup (1 stick) unsalted butter, softened
½ cup firmly packed dark brown sugar
½ cup firmly packed light brown sugar
2 large eggs
⅓ cup sour cream
⅔ cup buttermilk
1 heaping cup golden raisins

Preheat the oven to 350 degrees. Grease and flour a 9-inch square baking pan. If you want to turn cake out of the pan, line bottom with wax paper. Set aside.

Remove ¼ cup of the flour and set aside. Combine balance of the flour with the baking soda and powder, salt, and spices. Set aside.

Cream the butter and brown sugars until smooth, about 3 minutes. Add the eggs, 1 at a time, mixing well after each addition. Beat in the sour cream and buttermilk, then add the dry mixture and beat until smooth.

Dredge the raisins in the reserved ¼ cup of flour and fold into the batter (including any remaining flour). Pour batter into the prepared pan and bake for 35 to 45 minutes, or until a cake tester comes out clean. Let cool on cake rack.

Serves about 12

Nut Cake

Tucked into one of the few cookbooks my mother owned was this recipe from her friend Mrs. Block. I had never tried it before but remember having eaten it once at Mrs. Block's house during some Christmas season long ago. I'm glad it has survived. You'll like it!

4 cups sifted all-purpose flour
1 tablespoon baking powder
½ teaspoon salt
2 teaspoons ground cinnamon
1 tablespoon grated nutmeg
1 cup (2 sticks) unsalted butter, softened
2 cups sugar
6 medium eggs
4 cups coarsely chopped pecans
2 cups coarsely chopped English walnuts
2 cups coarsely chopped black walnuts
1 box (15 ounces) golden raisins
1 cup bourbon or dry white wine

Preheat the oven to 325 degrees. Grease and line the bottom of a 10-inch tube pan with wax paper. Grease the paper and flour the entire pan, shaking out excess. Set aside.

Set aside ½ cup of the flour and combine the balance with the baking powder, salt, cinnamon, and nutmeg. Sift together and set aside.

Cream the butter and sugar until fluffy, about 3 minutes. Beat in the eggs, 1 at the time, mixing well after each addition. Add dry mixture, mixing thoroughly.

Dredge nuts and raisins in the reserved ½ cup flour, then fold into the batter. Add the bourbon last and mix well. Pour batter into the prepared pan.

Bake for 1½ hours, or until top is hard and cake tester comes out clean. Be careful not to overbake, as this cake will dry out. Allow to cool completely in the pan before removing.

Serves 18 to 20

Left: White Fruitcake
Below: Zucchini Bread
Right: Sour Cream Pound Cake

Sticky Buns

These work fine as regular-size buns, but you might want to go wild and make them giant size—twice as big. And, I might add, sticky buns get their name honestly.

This recipe looks complicated, but really isn't. You will find these buns are easy to make while you are doing other things around the house, with all the elapsed time while the dough is rising. These are shown in the photograph opening the chapter.

> 1 package active dry yeast
> ¼ cup lukewarm water (105 to 115 degrees)
> 1 cup milk, scalded
> ¼ cup (½ stick) unsalted butter
> ¼ cup granulated sugar
> 1 teaspoon salt
> 1 large egg, lightly beaten
> 4 cups sifted all-purpose flour
>
> ### Caramel Nut Topping
> ¼ cup (½ stick) unsalted butter, melted
> ⅔ cup light corn syrup
> 1½ cups firmly packed light brown sugar
> 1 tablespoon ground cinnamon
> 1½ cups small pecan halves
>
> ### Filling
> 3 tablespoons unsalted butter, melted
> ½ cup firmly packed light brown sugar

Start by making the dough. Place the yeast in a small bowl and stir in the lukewarm water. Set aside for 10 minutes.

Pour the scalded milk over the butter, sugar, and salt in a large bowl. Mix well to dissolve the sugar and set aside to cool to lukewarm (105 to 115 degrees).

When milk has cooled, stir in yeast mixture and the beaten egg. Add the flour, ½ cup at the time, and stir to form a soft dough. Beat vigorously for a few minutes. Cover bowl with a damp tea towel and set aside in a warm, draft-free spot until dough rises to double its bulk, about 1½ to 2 hours.

Make the topping. When dough has risen, combine melted butter, syrup, brown sugar, and cinnamon in a small saucepan, preferably nonstick. Stir over low heat until smooth and sugar has dissolved.

Meanwhile, grease 16 regular muffin cups or 8 giant 4-inch cups. Divide the nuts evenly among the cups and then pour melted syrup over them. Set aside.

Divide dough in half, and roll one portion at a time out on a lightly floured board into a rectangle roughly 12 x 8 inches and about ¼ inch thick. Brush dough with half the melted butter for the filling and then sprinkle on half the brown sugar. Starting on one of the short sides, roll up dough jelly-roll fashion into a cylinder. Cut the cylinder into 8 equal slices. Place 1 slice, spiral side up, in each of 8 muffin cups. Repeat with the remaining portion of dough so all cups are filled.

Cover muffin tins with a damp cloth and allow dough to rise a second time until doubled, another 1½ to 2 hours.

When dough has almost finished rising the second time, preheat the oven to 375 degrees. Line a couple of jelly-roll pans or cookie sheets with foil and place the muffin tins on the pans before placing them in the oven. The sugar sometimes boils over the edges, and the pans make cleanup easier. Bake for 25 minutes, or until brown. Invert muffin tins onto a sheet of foil immediately and let cool.

Makes 16 regular or 8 giant buns

White Fruitcake

At last, the fabled "Windsor fruitcake." Nothing more need be said.

> 3 cups sifted all-purpose flour
> 1 teaspoon baking powder
> ¼ teaspoon salt
> 1½ teaspoons ground cinnamon
> 1 teaspoon ground allspice
> 1 teaspoon ground cloves
> 1 teaspoon grated nutmeg
> 1 cup (2 sticks) unsalted butter, softened
> 2 cups sugar
> 6 large eggs, well beaten
> ½ cup dry sherry
> 2 cups blanched almond halves
> 1½ cups coarsely chopped pecans
> ½ cup coarsely chopped walnuts
> 1 box (15 ounces) golden raisins
> 1½ cups diced candied citron
> 1½ cups diced candied pineapple
> ½ cup diced candied orange peel

Preheat the oven to 300 degrees. Grease a 10-inch tube pan and line the bottom with wax paper. Grease the paper and flour the inside of the entire pan. Set aside.

Sift together the flour, baking powder, salt, cinnamon, allspice, cloves, and nutmeg. Set aside.

Cream the butter and sugar until fluffy, about 3 minutes. Beat in the eggs thoroughly, then add the sherry and mix well. Mix in the nuts and fruits. Add the dry mixture in 4 parts, mixing thoroughly after each addition. Pour batter into the prepared pan.

Bake for approximately 2 hours, or until a cake tester comes out clean. Allow cake to cool in the pan, then loosen edges and invert onto a serving plate.

Makes 18 to 24 servings

Sour Cream Pound Cake

If moist and flavorful is what you want, this pound cake is the ticket—and it is simple to make. Also remember that pound cakes freeze extremely well and actually improve with a bit of age.

    1¾ cups sifted all-purpose flour
     ¼ teaspoon baking soda
     ½ cup (1 stick) unsalted butter, softened
    1½ cups sugar
     3 large eggs, separated, at room temperature
     ⅔ cup sour cream
     1 teaspoon vanilla extract

Preheat the oven to 325 degrees. Butter and flour a 9 x 5-inch loaf pan. Set aside.

Sift together the flour and baking soda. Set aside.

Cream the butter and sugar until fluffy, about 3 minutes. Add the eggs yolks and beat well.

Add one third of the flour mixture and beat to incorporate, then add the sour cream and beat again. Repeat until flour mixture and sour cream are mixed in. Stir in vanilla.

Beat egg whites until very stiff, then fold into the batter with an over-and-under motion. Pour into the prepared pan.

Bake on the center rack of the oven for about 1 hour 20 minutes, or until golden on top and a cake tester comes out clean.

Let cake cool in the pan on a rack. It can be stored in an airtight container or frozen (indefinitely).

Serves 12

Zucchini Bread

Noel Harrington has been making this for years. Thanks to him for letting us use his recipe.

If you have tender, fresh zucchini, leave the skins on. They add nice color. If the zucchini is less than just picked or is rather thick skinned, you might want to remove some or all of the skin. Use 1-pound coffee cans (with only one end removed) as your baking pans to make these perfectly round little loaves.

    3 cups sifted all-purpose flour
    2 teaspoons baking powder
    1 teaspoon baking soda
    1 tablespoon plus 2 teaspoons ground
       cinnamon
   2½ cups sugar
    ½ cup corn oil
    3 large eggs
    1 teaspoon vanilla extract
    2 cups grated or finely shredded zucchini
    1 cup coarsely chopped walnuts

Preheat the oven to 350 degrees. Grease and flour three 1-pound coffee cans or two 9 x 5-inch loaf pans. Set aside.

Sift together the flour, baking powder, baking soda, and cinnamon. Set aside.

Combine the sugar and oil and beat until sugar is somewhat dissolved. Add the eggs, 1 at a time, beating after each addition. Stir in the vanilla and zucchini, then add the dry mixture one third at the time. Mix very well, then stir in nuts. Divide batter among tins or loaf pans.

Bake for 1¼ hours, or until a cake tester comes out almost clean.

Allow loaves to cool in the cans on a wire rack. If the bread is reluctant to come out, open the other end of the can and push through.

Makes 3 small or 2 larger loaves

Puddings and Custards

Previous page: *Citrus Pudding Cake*

Puddings and custards must surely be the most soothing of all desserts. Their creamy texture and subtle flavor are a treat for the senses and palate. For that reason alone, they are a perfect way to finish almost any spicy, rich meal; this probably accounts for why flans are such popular desserts in Mexico and Spain. But texture and flavor aside, custards are also among the easiest desserts to make, being composed primarily of sweetened milk or cream with eggs.

Some custards are baked while others are cooked on top of the stove, and they can be either glamorous, like crème brûlée, or down-home, like bread pudding. I've included a few mousses and steamed puddings here as well.

Like most people, my introduction to these desserts came with my first banana pudding—or maybe it was that baked custard with a vanilla wafer in the bottom my grandmother used to make. I don't actually remember. That's the thing about custards. When you look back, you discover they were always just there.

However, I *do* remember my first crème brûlée. It must have been about 1951. I was living in New Orleans, and I was invited to dinner at the home of Margaret Williams, an imaginative hostess noted for her good parties and good food. And at the end of the meal, there it was: crème brûlée. I recall thinking at the time that it didn't look all that appetizing, even surrounded by plump fresh strawberries, but when I tasted it I was hooked.

Of course, crème brûlée had been a popular dessert long before then. And although everyone with any cooking skill in the Crescent City seemed able to make it with ease, for my part, I had the devil of a time learning how to do it.

While we are on the subject of New Orleans, that city must hold a record for the seemingly endless variations of bread pudding found in its restaurants. As a matter of fact, when friends are going there for their first visit and they ask me about places to dine, I often suggest that they compare bread puddings while they are at it. They always come back amazed.

Incidentally, I suddenly remembered it was at about this same time (1951) and at this same house (Margaret Williams's) that I had my first quiche. It didn't look too good either, but I sure liked it. If I had had any sense, I probably could have cornered the quiche market. Well, things sure have changed; anyway, that's another book.

It is a mark of the wonderful flexibility of custards and puddings that, with so few ingredients, there can be so many variations. Take flans, for instance. They look wonderful when unmolded; by flavoring with a bit of coffee, you get one kind (page 71) and by merely adding coconut (page 70), you get another, quite different, dessert. And, of course, even served plain, flans are hard to beat.

I have discovered one drawback, however. If custards or puddings are made too far in advance (by that I mean several days), their flavor tends to deteriorate somewhat. Custards and puddings must always be refrigerated because of their milk and egg content. Their delicate and appealing flavor seems to readily absorb other odors from the refrigerator, no matter how carefully wrapped.

And, speaking of refrigeration, always be sure your custard is completely cooled before you cover it to put in the refrigerator.

And don't forget that by using custard as part of a larger concoction you may create another kind of madness, as in custard-filled cakes (sunshine cream cake, page 34) or with that great English invention, the trifle, which closes this chapter. There is room for a lot of experimentation in this area, so use your imagination. When you do experiment, don't forget the value of a sprinkling of rum, brandy, or sherry to give your dessert a flavor kick and nuts to give it textural variety. And don't forget the whipped cream. What the hell? As long as you are at it, you might just as well go all the way.

Finally, let me repeat what I said at the beginning. An important consideration these days, when everyone seems to be on such a tight schedule, is that custards are so simple to prepare they may be made hours in advance of the time you will be serving them.

Also remember that, by varying sauces to complement and finish off a dessert as unassuming as honey custard (page 71), you can make numerous delectable fresh combinations. There is a whole section on sauces and toppings beginning on page 149.

Citrus Pudding Cake

This dessert can be made with either lemon, lime, or orange. Each is distinctive and delicious—and all are easy.

> 3 tablespoons unsalted butter
> 1 cup plus 2 tablespoons sugar
> 3 large eggs, separated, at room temperature
> ¼ cup less 2 tablespoons all-purpose flour
> 1½ cups milk
> ¼ cup plus 2 tablespoons lemon or lime juice (or ½ cup orange)
> 1 teaspoon grated citrus rind

Preheat the oven to 350 degrees. Generously butter a 1½-quart soufflé dish. Set aside.

Cream the butter and sugar until smooth, about 3 minutes. Add the egg yolks, 1 at a time, beating well after each addition. Stir in the flour and add the milk in 4 parts, mixing after each addition. Mix in citrus juice and grated rind.

Beat the egg whites until stiff, then fold into the mixture. Pour into the prepared soufflé dish and place soufflé dish in a larger pan. Surround dish with boiling water.

Bake for 1 hour, or until top is puffy.

Serve 6 to 8

Opposite: Berry Mousse. _Above:_ Bread Pudding II

Above: Arborio Rum-Raisin Rice Pudding; Butterscotch Pudding. _Below:_ Bread Pudding I

Arborio Rum-Raisin Rice Pudding

Ina Garten, the inspiration behind the Barefoot Contessa stores in Long Island's Hamptons, came up with this variation on an old favorite. It's rich as all get out, so a little bit goes a long way—but so good.

1	cup Arborio (Italian) rice
5	cups half-and-half
½	cup sugar
1½	teaspoons vanilla extract
	Seeds of 1 vanilla bean*
½	cup golden raisins
1	large egg, lightly beaten
1	cup heavy cream
¼	cup dark rum

Combine the rice, half-and-half, sugar, vanilla, vanilla seeds, and raisins in a large saucepan set over low heat. Simmer for about 25 minutes, or until rice is al dente. Add the egg and cook for just another minute or 2 to thicken.

Off the heat, add the cream and rum. Mix well and chill before serving.

Serves 6

* Ina says she makes vanilla extract and softened vanilla beans by soaking them in vodka for a month or more. Then, when she wants the seeds, she just snips off the end of a bean and squeezes them out. She keeps this brew going for years, adding more vodka and beans as needed.

Berry Mousse

Almost any kind of berry can be used here, or make this a combination of anything handy. And, of course, berry juice of any kind stains the mousse a lovely color.

6	large eggs, separated, at room temperature
½	cup sugar
1	tablespoon unflavored gelatin
1	cup strained puréed raspberries
2	tablespoons kirsch or framboise
1	cup heavy cream
¼	cup sifted confectioners' sugar
¼	teaspoon cream of tartar
¼	teaspoon salt

Garnish
Fresh raspberries or Berry Sauce (page 151)

Place the yolks, sugar, and gelatin in a bowl and beat until light and thick. Put mixture in the top of a double boiler and stir in the raspberry purée. Cook over barely simmering water just long enough to dissolve the sugar and gelatin, then set aside to cool.

To assemble, put an oiled wax-paper collar around a 6-cup soufflé dish (or, if you don't want to bother with the collar, use a slightly larger dish) and stir the kirsch into the egg-raspberry mixture. Whip the cream, adding confectioners' sugar 1 tablespoon at a time, until stiff. Fold the cream into the raspberry mixture.

Beat the egg whites until foamy. Add the cream of tartar and salt and continue beating until soft peaks form. Fold the whites into the other mixture and pour into the prepared soufflé dish. Refrigerate for several hours or until set.

Serve the mousse topped with additional berries and puréed berry sauce, if desired.

Serves 6 to 8

Bread Pudding I

One of my all-time favorite desserts. And a "crowd pleaser," I might add.

10	or more 1-inch-thick slices day-old French bread, with crusts trimmed
½	cup (1 stick) unsalted butter, softened
4	large eggs
¾	cup plus 2 tablespoons sugar
4	cups milk
2	tablespoons vanilla extract
	Freshly grated nutmeg
	Whipped cream flavored with bourbon or liqueur

Preheat the oven to 350 degrees. Generously butter a 6-cup soufflé dish or low oval baking dish. Set aside.

Spread bread slices generously with the softened butter and place, buttered side up, in the baking dish. There should be enough pieces to cover the bottom.

Beat the eggs and ¾ cup of sugar until smooth. Pour milk in while stirring, then add vanilla and nutmeg. Mix very well.

Carefully pour the mixture through a strainer into the baking dish. Sprinkle the tops of the bread slices with the remaining 2 tablespoons of sugar.

Place dish in a larger ovenproof pan and surround with hot water.

Reduce the oven heat to 325 degrees and bake for 45 minutes, or until set. (Pudding will be a little jiggly when you remove it from the oven, but will set when refrigerated.)

Serve with flavored whipped cream.

Serves 6 to 8

Bread Pudding II

The second bread pudding is not designated such because I feel it is inferior to the first one. Rather, the second is a more down-home version of the same, with enough difference to make it distinctive. This recipe came to me courtesy of Joel English, who supervises the cooking at Mandich Restaurant, which she and her husband run together. Mandich's is in New Orleans, a city where, as I said in the introduction to this chapter, they know all about bread pudding.

    4 large eggs
    1 cup sugar
    ¼ cup (½ stick) unsalted butter, melted
    1 quart milk
    1 tablespoon vanilla extract
    1 24-inch loaf stale French bread
    ½ cup raisins
    ½ cup canned fruit cocktail, drained
       Whiskey Sauce (recipe follows)

Preheat the oven to 350 degrees. Generously butter a 6-cup soufflé dish or oval baking dish. Set aside.

Mix the eggs, sugar, and melted butter in a large bowl. Add the milk and vanilla and mix well. Break the bread into small chunks and put into the mixture. When bread has softened, break into small bits with your hands and let it continue to soak until all the milk is absorbed. Fold in raisins and fruit cocktail. Pour mixture into the prepared dish and place dish into a larger ovenproof pan. Surround with boiling water, and bake about 1 hour and 15 minutes, or until firm and brown on top.

Serve with whiskey sauce.

Serves 8

Whiskey Sauce

    ½ cup (1 stick) butter, cut into small pieces
    1 cup sugar
    1 large egg
    ½ cup bourbon

Melt the butter in the top of a double boiler over hot, but not boiling, water. Mix the sugar and egg together, then add to melted butter. Stir to combine, then cook for 3 or 4 minutes, stirring, until sugar is dissolved and egg is cooked. Don't let the water underneath boil, or the egg will curdle. Remove sauce from the heat and let cool before stirring in the bourbon.

Makes about 2 cups

Butterscotch Pudding

This is real butterscotch pudding because it has Scotch whiskey in it!

    6 tablespoons (¾ stick) unsalted butter
    1¼ cups firmly packed dark brown sugar
    3 cups milk
    ¼ cup plus 2 tablespoons cornstarch
    ½ teaspoon salt
    3 large egg yolks, lightly beaten
    1 teaspoon vanilla extract
    3 tablespoons mild Scotch whiskey
    ½ cup chopped walnuts (optional)
       Whipped cream flavored with vanilla
       (optional)

Combine the butter and brown sugar in a large saucepan and cook over moderate heat until smooth. Add 2 ½ cups of the milk and continue to cook until steam rises from the surface.

Meanwhile, mix remaining ½ cup milk with the cornstarch and salt. Stir until smooth, then add to the butter mixture. Cook, stirring, until very thick, about 10 minutes.

Stir about ½ cup of the warm mixture into the egg yolks to warm them, then stir warmed yolks into the pudding. Cook for 3 minutes, stirring.

Remove from the heat and add the vanilla and whiskey (and walnuts, if desired). Pour into individual glasses and chill. Puddings may be topped with a dab of flavored whipped cream.

Serves 4 to 6

Clockwise from left:
Chutney Steamed Pudding;
Coconut and Espresso
Flans; Honey Custard;
Chocolate Soufflé
Opposite: Chocolate
Steamed Pudding

Chocolate Soufflé

This is Edna Lewis's famous recipe, which she kindly said we might use. One of the best—like its originator.

    4 ounces unsweetened chocolate
    1 cup milk
    1 4-inch piece of vanilla bean, split; or 1
      teaspoon good vanilla extract
    3 tablespoons unsalted butter
    2 tablespoons all-purpose flour
    ⅓ cup hot water
    2 large egg yolks
    ¼ teaspoon salt
    3 tablespoons granulated sugar
    5 large egg whites, at room temperature
    3 tablespoons confectioners' sugar
      Whipped cream

Preheat the oven to 400 degrees.

Grate the chocolate on the medium side of a grater. Set aside.

Heat the milk with the split vanilla bean over low heat and allow to steep while completing next step.

Melt the butter in a large, heavy saucepan, then stir in the flour, using a whisk. Remove the vanilla bean from the milk and add milk to the butter-flour mixture, stirring rapidly with a whisk. When thickened and smooth, remove saucepan from heat and add the grated chocolate. Stir well and add hot water, stirring all the while. (If vanilla extract is used instead of vanilla bean, add it here.)

Beat the egg yolks with the salt and granulated sugar until light and creamy, about 3 minutes. Stir yolk mixture into the chocolate mixture. Return saucepan to the heat and cook, stirring constantly, for 5 minutes. The mixture will look smooth and satiny when ready. Allow to cool slightly.

Beat the egg whites until stiff but not dry. Pour the chocolate sauce over the whites and fold the two together.

Spoon mixture into an ungreased 2-quart soufflé dish (or individual dishes).

Place immediately in the oven and increase heat to 450 degrees. Bake for 20 minutes (bake individual dishes for 12 or 13 minutes), or until puffed. Dust soufflé with confectioners' sugar and serve immediately with a chocolate sauce and whipped cream.

Serves 4 to 6

Chutney Steamed Pudding

I wish more people would serve steamed puddings; they are easy to make and are delightful.

    1 cup sifted all-purpose flour
    ½ teaspoon baking soda
    ½ cup (1 stick) unsalted butter, softened
    ½ cup firmly packed dark brown sugar
    2 large eggs
    ⅓ cup minced chutney
    ⅓ cup chopped walnuts
      Whipped cream flavored with vanilla or
      brandy
      Vanilla Custard Sauce (page 151)

Butter a 4-cup pudding mold (with a top). Set aside.

Sift the flour and soda together and set aside. Cream the butter and brown sugar until smooth, about 3 minutes. Add the eggs, 1 at the time, beating well after each addition. Beat in the dry mixture, then fold in chutney and nuts. Pour into prepared mold.

Cover securely and place mold in a larger pot (with a lid). Surround mold with hot water halfway up sides and place lid on pot. Simmer for 1½ hours, or until pudding has risen to top of mold. Cool for about 15 minutes before serving, and accompany with flavored cream or vanilla sauce.

Serves 6

Coconut Flan

Flans are a snap to make and may be varied simply by serving them with various sauces or fruits. Of course, they are perfectly fine too without any accompaniment.

    ¾ cup sugar
    2 tablespoons water
    4 large eggs, plus 1 egg yolk, at room
      temperature
    2 cups milk
    1 cup heavy cream
    ½ cup shredded fresh coconut (or more)

Preheat the oven to 300 degrees.

Mix ½ cup of the sugar with the water in a saucepan and bring to a boil over medium heat. Continue cooking until the mixture begins to caramelize, stirring all the while with a wooden spoon. When it is dark golden, pour into a 4½- or 6-cup ring mold. Using a pot holder (or metal tongs) to hold it, tilt the mold to coat the inside. Continue tilting and turning until the liquid sets. Set aside.

Lightly beat together the whole eggs and egg yolk. Set aside.

Scald the milk and cream together in a large saucepan. Lightly beat the remaining ¼ cup sugar into the eggs. Put a few tablespoons of the milk mixture into the egg mixture to heat it, then add warmed eggs to the milk. Mix well.

Sprinkle the coconut into the prepared mold and strain the cream mixture through a sieve into it. Place mold in a roasting pan, surround with hot water, and bake for about 50 minutes, or until set.

Allow to cool, then cover and refrigerate. Flan should be served cold.

Serves 6 to 8

Variation: To make espresso flan, omit the coconut and add a tablespoon of powdered instant espresso to the mixture before pouring it into the mold. Serve in a pool of Irish coffee sauce, page 151.

Chocolate Steamed Pudding

Mrs. John Thomas of Austin, Texas, had this recipe with her when she was still Mary Fulton Berry. That was at the turn of the century, when she was brought from Scotland to America by her family.

  1 cup sifted all-purpose flour
  2 teaspoons baking powder
  1 tablespoon butter, melted
  ½ cup sugar
  1 large egg, lightly beaten
1½ ounces semisweet chocolate, melted and slightly cooled
  ½ cup milk
    Bourbon Cream Sauce (recipe follows)

Generously butter a 4-cup mold with a lid, set aside.

Sift together the flour and baking powder. Set aside. Combine the melted butter and sugar, beating well, then add the egg and continue to beat until mixed. Stir in the melted chocolate and add the flour in 3 parts, alternating with the milk. Mix well, then pour into the prepared mold.

Place lid securely on the mold and put mold into a larger pot. Surround mold halfway up with hot water. Cover the pot and steam the pudding over low heat for 1 hour. Allow pudding to rest for about 15 minutes before serving with the cream sauce.

Serves 4 to 6

Bourbon Cream Sauce

  2 large eggs, separated, at room temperature
  1 cup sifted confectioners' sugar
  ½ cup heavy cream, whipped
  1 tablespoon bourbon

Beat the yolks with the confectioners' sugar until smooth. Fold in the whipped cream and set aside. Beat the egg whites until they make soft peaks, then fold into the cream mixture. Stir in bourbon.

Makes about 2 cups

Honey Custard

I bet you will be surprised at how tasty this very easy little custard is. You'll probably make it often once you give it a try.

  2 cups milk
  ¼ cup honey
  1 teaspoon vanilla extract
  3 large eggs
    Pinch of salt
    Grinding of nutmeg or sprinkling of cinnamon
    Berry Sauce (page 151) or flavored whipped cream (page 150)

Preheat the oven to 375 degrees. Generously butter 6 individual ½-cup custard cups. Set aside.

Scald the milk, being careful not to scorch it. Off the heat, stir in the honey and then the vanilla. Beat the eggs and salt together, then stir in several tablespoons of the milk mixture to warm the eggs. While continuing to stir, pour the warmed eggs into the milk. Add the nutmeg or cinnamon and strain through a sieve into the prepared cups. Place cups in a shallow baking pan and surround with boiling water.

Bake custards for 40 minutes, or until a knife inserted into the center comes out clean. Allow to cool (out of the water). Refrigerate covered.

Serve in the cups, or unmold the custards by running a knife around the edge of each, inverting them over individual plates, and, holding them in place firmly, giving them a sharp downward shake. Top with a berry sauce or flavored whipped cream.

Serves 6

Opposite: Trifle
Top: Jubilee Custard
with Cherry Sauce
Above: Summer Pudding
Right: Tangerine Mousse

Jubilee Custard

Sherrye Henry told me this is one of the family recipes she took with her from Tennessee when she got married. It makes a beautiful dessert that tastes as good as it looks.

    1   envelope unflavored gelatin
    3   tablespoons cold water
    1¼ cups milk
        Dash of salt
    2   large eggs, separated, at room temperature
    1   teaspoon vanilla extract
    ¼   cup sugar
    1   cup heavy cream
        Cherry Sauce (recipe follows)

Stir gelatin into the 3 tablespoons cold water and set aside. While gelatin is dissolving, combine milk and salt in a double boiler and heat slowly.

Meanwhile, lightly beat the egg yolks and stir in a few tablespoons of the heated milk to warm them. Stirring all the while, slowly pour the warmed yolks into the milk and continue to cook, stirring, over barely boiling water until slightly thickened. Add the softened gelatin and stir until completely dissolved. Remove from the heat and add the vanilla. Mix and allow to cool until just beginning to thicken.

Beat the egg whites until stiff, adding the sugar 1 tablespoon at a time. Set aside for a minute while you whip the cream. Fold the beaten egg whites and whipped cream into the custard mixture. Coat the inside of a 5-cup mold with vegetable cooking spray and pour custard in. Refrigerate until set.

To serve, unmold (this may take a firm shake, as with the honey custard) and accompany with cherry sauce.

Serves 8

Cherry Sauce

    1   can (17 ounces) pitted black cherries,
         drained, reserving syrup
         2-inch strip lemon peel
    1   tablespoon fresh lemon juice
    1½   tablespoons cornstarch
    2   tablespoons water
    1   cup halved strawberries (optional)

Place the reserved cherry syrup in a medium saucepan and add the peel and lemon juice. Set aside.

In a small bowl, mix the cornstarch with the water and stir until smooth. Stir this into the syrup and cook over medium heat, stirring all the while, until mixture is clear and thickened, about 10 minutes. Add the cherries off the heat and allow to cool. Just before serving, mix in strawberries, if desired.

Makes about 2 cups

Summer Pudding

I had never made a summer pudding until several years ago, but now I am a convert. I think you will be too, if you aren't already. Use almost any combination of berries you have on hand; here, I use a combination of blueberries and strawberries.

    1½   pounds combined blueberries and
         strawberries
         Grated peel of 1 lemon
    ¼   cup plus 2 tablespoons sugar
    5   or more slices white bread, crusts trimmed
         Whipped cream flavored with vanilla extract

Remove stems and pick over berries, cutting the strawberries in half. Combine fruit with the lemon peel and sugar in a small nonaluminum saucepan. Cover and simmer for 10 minutes. Take care, lest the whole thing boil over when it starts to cook.

Cut each slice of bread into 3 strips and line the bottom and sides of a 4-cup soufflé dish (patching with pieces of bread if necessary). Strain the fruit pulp, reserving the juice. Pour several tablespoons of the juice over the bottom slices of bread and let it set for a few minutes.

Fill the soufflé dish almost to the top with fruit

pulp, then pour in enough juice to moisten. Cover top with a layer of bread and dampen this with a little juice, too. Put a small plate, which just fits inside the dish, on top and wrap the whole thing in cling wrap. Set on a plate in the refrigerator with a weight on top. (A large can may be used as a weight.) Leave for 24 hours.

To serve, run a knife around the edges and invert the dish onto a serving platter, being careful not to spill the accumulated juice. If juice has not stained all the bread through, you may do so with the reserved juice.

Serve with whipped cream and reserved juice.

Serves 4 to 6

Trifle

I find trifles almost irresistible. Like other such desserts, I save them for special occasions because they are so rich—but what a treat they are!

    1 loaf day-old pound cake, cut into thick slices
    ¾ cup raspberry, blackberry, strawberry, or
       currant jam, seedless
    ¼ cup slivered almonds
    ½ cup grated fresh coconut (optional)
    ½ cup dry sherry
    ¼ cup plus 2 tablespoons brandy
    2 cups half-and-half
    1 teaspoon cornstarch
    3 tablespoons sugar
    5 large egg yolks, well beaten
    1½ teaspoons vanilla extract
    2 cups heavy cream, whipped

    Garnish
    Whole almonds and/or strawberries
    (optional)

Select a large glass bowl and arrange cake slices to completely cover the bottom (you may cut pieces to patch with). Spread thickly with the jam, then sprinkle with a few slivered almonds and the coconut, if desired. Sprinkle generously with the sherry and brandy. Set aside.

In the top of a double boiler, heat the half-and-half to the point of boiling. Remove from the heat. Mix the cornstarch and sugar together, then stir this into the egg yolks. Add a few tablespoons of the hot half-and-half to the yolks to warm them, then a few more tablespoons to make the mixture liquid and pourable.

Back on the heat (over barely simmering water), pour the warmed yolks into the cream, stirring all the while. Continue to cook until custard becomes thick and smooth. Don't let it boil, since this will cause it to curdle. Off the heat, stir in the vanilla.

Allow the custard to cool, then pour a heavy layer over the cake in the bowl. Make another layer of cake, followed by the jam and so on as before, then cover with more custard. When you have used up all the ingredients (except the whipped cream and optional almonds and strawberries), top with whipped cream and garnish with nuts and fruit.

Cover and allow to chill in the refrigerator for at least half a day before serving, to let flavors meld.

Additional fresh fruit, nuts, and/or coconut may be sprinkled on top.

Serves 8 to 12

Tangerine Mousse

Another dessert that is extremely easy to put together, this mousse makes a very tempting presentation. Serve it with a few berries or peeled tangerine slices on top, if you like.

    1 envelope unflavored gelatin
    ¼ cup cold water
    ¾ cup frozen tangerine concentrate, thawed
       but not diluted
    ½ cup sugar
       Pinch of salt
    1 tablespoon lemon juice
    2 cups heavy cream, whipped

In a small nonaluminum saucepan, sprinkle the gelatin over the water and allow to soften for a few minutes. Add the tangerine concentrate, sugar, salt, and lemon juice. Stir to mix well, and simmer over moderate heat until sugar and gelatin dissolve, about 3 to 5 minutes. Allow to cool and thicken a bit.

Stir 2 tablespoons of the tangerine mixture into ¾ cup of the whipped cream and set aside. Fold remaining tangerine mixture into the remaining whipped cream, mixing well. Spoon the larger tangerine mixture into individual serving dishes or 1 large one. Spoon equal amounts of the reserved whipped cream onto the top of each serving to make a pattern. Chill until set.

Serves 6

Cobblers and the Like

Previous page: Blackberry Cobbler

M y guess is that this category includes what probably must have been the mainstay desserts during America's early days, when the country was still a wild and frontier place. Cobblers and crisps are among the simplest and most direct sweets, being little more than fruit with a crust (when the cook had time) or with a crumble topping (when the cook didn't). The ingredients probably were also usually available. And together, their flavor was hardy and rewarding —just the sort of thing people need after a hard day of carving out a new life for themselves and their families.

In the final analysis, almost any sort of fruit could have been—and can be—used: apples, pears, peaches, plums, quince, apricots, along with the berries that must have grown everywhere a hundred and fifty years ago. And in winter, when the apples finally gave out or were running low, stored fruit from the cellar could have been combined with dried fruit to come up with something almost as tasty as the genuine fresh article.

So the cobbler is a dessert with no secrets except its simplicity. And, ironically, that very characteristic is the one most often at risk from overzealous cooks who try to fancy cobblers up with the addition of too many kinds of spices, thickening agents, flavorings, and complicated crusts.

Years ago, I wanted to make a blackberry cobbler for the first time (still my favorite); in an effort to re-create the elusive flavor I recalled so vividly from my childhood, I turned to a number of different recipes. By a process of trial and disappointment, I figured out the crust, but it took longer to get around to leaving everything out of the filling except the fruit, butter, and sugar. And it was finally Edna Lewis who made me see the light. When I tried her cobbler, it tasted just like the ones I grew up with.

So do yourself a favor. If you like cobblers, experiment a little but stick to very few ingredients. And whenever you see too many ingredients in a cobbler recipe, put the whole thing down to a cookbook writer's ego (or desperation)—and move on.

Blackberry Cobbler

During blackberry season I always pick extras to freeze so I can have at least an approximation of this, my favorite of all cobblers, after fresh berries are gone. Admittedly, it is not as tasty when made with frozen berries, but in the dead of winter, it comes close enough.

> 1½ cups sifted all-purpose flour
> Scant ¼ teaspoon salt
> 5 tablespoons solid vegetable shortening, frozen
> ¼ cup (½ stick) unsalted butter, frozen
> 4 to 5 tablespoons ice water
> 6 cups fresh blackberries, washed and drained
> ¾ cup sugar
> ¼ cup (½ stick) unsalted butter, cut into bits
> Sugar for sprinkling, or crushed sugar cubes
> Whipped cream or ice cream

Preheat the oven to 425 degrees. Have ready a 9-inch round ovenproof dish that is 2 or more inches deep.

Combine the flour, salt, and frozen shortening and butter in a food processor fitted with a metal blade. Process until the mixture is rough textured. Add the water slowly, and process until the dough begins to cling together. Gather into a ball and place between 2 sheets of wax paper, flattening the ball slightly. Refrigerate for 30 minutes.

Roll the dough out on a floured surface into a large, ragged circle about 15 inches in diameter. Then roll the circle up onto the rolling pin, window-shade fashion. Unroll the crust over the baking dish and line the bottom and sides, allowing the excess crust to drape over the edge. Mound the berries in the middle, and sprinkle with the sugar and dot with the butter pieces. Bring the pastry crust up over berries; it will not quite cover the fruit, but use any pieces that have fallen off to patch. Sprinkle the top of the dough with a little more sugar or, like Edna Lewis, sprinkle crushed sugar cubes on top.

Bake for 45 minutes, or until the crust is brown and the filling is bubbling. Serve with whipped cream or ice cream.

Serves 6 to 8

Apple Dumplings with Almond Sauce

This recipe, which I have varied only slightly, came to me from Mrs. Yvonne LeBoeuf of Houma, Louisiana, who said it has been in her family for over a hundred years.

The dumpling dough is very stiff and dense, it works and probably must be that way to keep it from dissolving during the cooking time.

The very limited number of ingredients called for here is typical of many old desserts, which I imagine were put together simply from whatever was handy—before we all got so fancy about everything.

>   3 cups coarsely chopped, peeled tart apples
>   Grated rind of 1 lemon
> 3¾ cups sifted all-purpose flour
> 1½ tablespoons baking powder
>   ¾ cup cold milk
>   2 large eggs, lightly beaten
>   Whipped cream flavored with vanilla (optional)
>
>   ***Almond Sauce***
>   4 cups water
>   ½ cup (1 stick) unsalted butter
>   ½ cup (1 stick) margarine
>   ¾ cup sugar
>   Pinch of salt
>   ¾ teaspoon vanilla extract
>   ¾ cup slivered almonds

Preheat the oven to 350 degrees.

Combine the chopped apples and lemon rind in a bowl. Set aside.

Sift the flour and baking powder into the bowl of a food processor fitted with a steel blade. Combine the milk and eggs and add to flour all at once. Process until the mixture clings together and forms a ball. This makes a *very* stiff dough. Roll out dough on a floured surface until very thin. Cut dough into twelve 4-inch squares and place a tablespoon of the apple mixture in the middle of each. Bring the 4 corners of each square together, slightly twisting and squeezing to seal. Make 12 dumplings, discarding any scraps of dough.* Place dumplings in a deep 9- to 10-inch baking dish or ovenproof casserole, squeezing together if necessary. Sprinkle leftover chopped apple over all and set aside.

To make the sauce, bring the water to a boil in a medium saucepan and add the butter, margarine, sugar, salt, and vanilla. Cook until dissolved. Sprinkle almonds over the dumplings and then pour liquid over dumplings.

Bake, uncovered, about 1 hour, or until the dumplings are golden and the sauce is reduced. Serve dumplings with sauce spooned over each portion. They may also be topped with flavored whipped cream.

Serves 6 to 12

* Since this dough is so stiff and dry, it is hard to utilize the scraps for rerolling. I have purposely made the quantity of dough generous to account for this.

Peach Crumble Cake

Crumble cake is typically easy to make and may be varied by changing the fruit and the spices, so let your imagination be your guide.

As with the peach cobbler, this dessert should really only be made when tree-ripened (in season) peaches can be had, because the success of it depends so much on the fruit's natural flavor.

>   ½ cup (1 stick) unsalted butter, softened
>   ½ cup firmly packed light brown sugar
>   ½ cup plus 3 tablespoons granulated sugar
>   1 cup sifted all-purpose flour
>   1 teaspoon baking powder
>   2 large eggs
> 10 large peaches, skinned, pitted, and cut in half
>   1 tablespoon fresh lemon juice
>   ½ teaspoon ground cinnamon
>   Vanilla-flavored whipped cream or ice cream

Preheat the oven to 350 degrees. Lightly butter an 8-inch square baking dish. Set aside.

Cream the butter, brown sugar, and ½ cup of granulated sugar until light and fluffy, about 3 minutes. Sift together the flour and baking powder, then beat into the butter mixture. Beat in eggs.

Scrape the mixture into the prepared baking dish and place the peach halves on top of the batter, flat side down. Sprinkle with the lemon juice (more if you like). Mix the remaining sugar with the cinnamon and sprinkle it over the peaches (You may also increase this amount if you like).

Bake for 1 hour, or until golden. Serve with flavored whipped cream or ice cream.

Serves 6 to 8

<u>Above, left to right:</u> *Apple-Calvados Cherry Crisp; Apple Dumplings with Almond Sauce; Blueberry Brown Betty*

Below, left to right: Peach Cobbler; Buttermilk-Plum Cobbler; Pear-Raspberry Cobbler

Buttermilk-Plum Cobbler

The quantity of plums here is fairly flexible. I have called for a dozen large ones; obviously if they are not big, you would want more. You can't really go too wrong with this easy recipe.

- 12 large unpeeled plums, washed, pitted, and cut into 8 pieces
- ¾ cup firmly packed light brown sugar (or less)
- 7 tablespoons unsalted butter
  Juice of ¼ lemon
- 1 cup sifted all-purpose flour
- 1 teaspoon baking powder
- ¼ teaspoon baking soda
- ½ teaspoon salt
- ¾ cup buttermilk
  Whipped cream or ice cream

Preheat the oven to 425 degrees. Butter a deep 7 x 9-inch ovenproof dish. Set aside.

Mix the plums and sugar and spread evenly in the dish. Dot with 4 tablespoons of the butter and squeeze the lemon juice over all. Bake, uncovered, for 25 minutes.

Meanwhile, sift together the flour, baking powder, baking soda, and salt. Cut in the remaining 3 tablespoons butter with a pastry blender or 2 knives. When plums are baked, stir the buttermilk into the dry ingredients and drop by large tablespoonfuls onto the plums. Bake an additional 25 minutes, or until biscuits have browned.

Serve warm or at room temperature with whipped cream or ice cream.

Serves 6 to 8

Peach Cobbler

I only make this dessert during the height of the local peach season, for, as you can see by the ingredients, the cobbler's flavor depends almost entirely on the flavor of the fruit. Out-of-season peaches, no matter how tempting they may look, just don't do the trick.

Because this is very juicy, it is best served in shallow bowls.

- 1½ cups sifted all-purpose flour
  Scant ¼ teaspoon salt
- 5 tablespoons unsalted butter, frozen
- ¼ cup solid vegetable shortening, frozen
- 5 tablespoons ice water
- 7 very large ripe peaches, skinned and pitted
- 1 cup sugar
- ¼ cup (½ stick) unsalted butter, cut into bits
  Whipped cream or ice cream

Preheat the oven to 450 degrees. Lightly grease a deep 7 x 9-inch ovenproof dish. Set aside.

Place the flour and salt in the bowl of a food processor fitted with a metal blade. Add the frozen butter and shortening. Process until mixture is the size of small peas. Add ice water and process until mixture begins to form a ball. Remove and shape into a ball. If you would like to refrigerate the dough at this point, flatten between 2 sheets of wax paper. Meanwhile, cut the peaches into thick slices and set aside.

To assemble the cobbler, roll the dough out into a large, ragged rectangle on a floured surface. Dust with flour and roll back onto the rolling pin, window-shade fashion. Unroll over the prepared dish, lining the bottom and sides and allowing excess dough to hang over sides. Heap peaches into the dish. Sprinkle with the sugar and dot with the butter pieces. Flop the loose ends of the pastry over the top, using any pieces that might have fallen off as patches.

Put cobbler into the oven and turn temperature to 425 degrees. Bake for 45 minutes, or until top is golden. Serve with whipped cream or ice cream.

Serves 6

Blueberry Brown Betty

Some recipes for brown betty call for finely ground toasted bread crumbs, but I much prefer large soft bread crumbs (made from protein bread). You can make these crumbs in a food processor or pinch off small pieces of bread by hand.

    6 cups washed fresh blueberries
    ½ cup firmly packed brown sugar
    ½ teaspoon ground cinnamon
       Grated rind and juice of ½ large lemon
    2 heaping cups coarse fresh bread crumbs
    ⅓ cup butter, melted
       Cream or ice cream

Preheat the oven to 350 degrees. Butter a deep 7 x 9-inch ovenproof dish and set aside.

Mix the berries, brown sugar, cinnamon, lemon rind, and juice. Pour half the berries into the prepared dish. Toss the bread crumbs with the melted butter and spread half over the berries in the dish. Top with the remaining berries and then the remaining crumbs, smoothing the surface.

Bake for 30 minutes, then cover lightly with a piece of foil and bake an additional 15 minutes until blueberries are bubbling.

Serve warm with cream or ice cream.

Serves 6 to 8

Apple-Calvados Cherry Crisp

Apples are about the best year-round staple for making baked fruit desserts. Here they are joined by wonderful dried tart cherries soaked in calvados (apple brandy)—a nice twist on an old standby.

    6 ounces dried tart cherries*
    ⅓ cup calvados
       Approximately 6 cups sliced, peeled, and cored apples, such as granny smith or mcintosh
    1 cup sifted all-purpose flour
    ¾ cup sugar
    ½ teaspoon ground cinnamon
    ¼ teaspoon salt
    ½ cup (1 stick) unsalted butter, softened and cut into bits
       Whipped cream flavored with vanilla extract or vanilla ice cream

Preheat the oven to 350 degrees. Combine the dried cherries with the calvados and set aside for at least 10 minutes.

Mix marinated cherries (and remaining calvados) with the apples and place evenly in a deep 7 x 9-inch greased baking dish. Combine remaining ingredients and mix with your hands until mixture is the texture of rough meal. Spread evenly over the apples, smoothing with your hand.

Bake for approximately 35 minutes, or until the top begins to turn color and the mixture is bubbling. Serve with flavored whipped cream or ice cream.

Serves 6 to 8

* Dried tart cherries may be purchased directly from American Spoon Foods, Petoskey, Michigan 49770; or American Spoon Foods will tell you if dried cherries are available in your area.

Pear-Raspberry Cobbler

Pears and raspberries are a luscious combination, with one fruit complementing the other perfectly. And this dish looks as good as it tastes.

    1   recipe for Cobbler Dough (page 78)
    6   cups peeled, cored, and sliced firm pears
    1¼ cups fresh raspberries (or frozen, in a pinch)
    ¾   cup sugar
    ¼   cup (½ stick) unsalted butter, cut into bits
        Cream or ice cream

Preheat the oven to 425 degrees. Grease a deep 7 x 9-inch ovenproof dish. Set aside.

Roll out dough into a rough rectangle and line pan as in the peach cobbler, letting excess crust drape over the edge. Heap pears into dish, mounding slightly in the middle. Sprinkle the berries evenly over dish and then pour sugar evenly over all. Dot with butter. Bring dough up and let it flop over fruit, using any that falls off to patch in the middle.

Bake for 45 minutes, or until golden brown. Serve with cream or ice cream.

Serves 6 to 8

Apple Pie

Apple and Green Tomato Tart

Blueberry Pie

Butterscotch Pie

Chess Pie

Chocolate Cream Pie
with Chocolate Meringue

Coconut Cream Pie

Impossible Pie

Lemon Meringue Pie

Macadamia Cream Pie

Osgood Pie

Pear Tart

Pumpkin Chiffon Pie

Rhubarb Pie

Strawberry Pie

Sugar Tart

Walnut Tart

Pies and Tarts

I n season, the Hamptons on Long Island, where my house is, must be the fruit-pie capital of the nation. Pies seem to be sold at every market and vegetable stand, probably because fresh fruit is so readily available and the pies are so easy to make. And, once made, they hold well. As a matter of fact, I would guess that in many people's minds (out there, at least), these pies have come to be almost synonymous with country desserts. I know I've certainly eaten my share of them at friends' houses on the weekends.

Well, not to be a sorehead, but I've never quite understood why, since they *are* so easy to make, people don't bake the pies themselves instead of buying them. The flavor and texture of a fresh homemade pie are a hundred times better than those that have been baked long hours in advance of when they are to be served.

All you have to do is learn to make and handle pie dough, which—with a food processor and two sheets of wax paper—is a snap. With the food processor to mix the dough, this job takes exactly as long as the time required to give the blades a few whirls. The dough is then gathered into a ball, flattened slightly, and refrigerated for fifteen or twenty minutes—or a day. When it comes to assembling the pie, take the dough out and let it rest at room temperature for thirty minutes or so if it has been in the refrigerator for long, then tear off two pieces of wax paper. Dust the dough lightly with flour on all sides, brushing off the excess. Place it between the two sheets of paper and roll it out. Peel off the top sheet when the dough is the right thickness, then invert it onto the pie pan with the second piece of

wax paper still adhering. Peel this off when the pastry is properly positioned. Carefully ease the dough into the pan and cut off the edges. Fill the pie and put the top crust on, preparing it the same way you did the bottom one. Crimp the edges and bake. The hot-water crust on page 90 is very stable and easy to work with. It freezes well, too, so while you are at it, make enough for two pies and freeze one.

If you are filling a pie crust with custard or cream, prebake the crust and be sure to use pie weights or dried beans so the crust will keep its shape. And even after you remove the weights, check it a time or two to puncture any bubbles that may form in the dough as it is baking. This will in no way harm the crust, but will assure that the crust remains flat in the pan.

And while we are on the subject of pie crusts, don't forget that it may be made from things other than dough. There are crusts made from nuts, like the truly marvelous-tasting macadamia crust on page 98, as well as the coconut, gingersnap, and vanilla-wafer crusts also found in this chapter. Once you learn to make these, you might want to experiment with different fillings and different crusts. For instance, when we made the macadamia crust to photograph, we made an extra in case we had a mishap—and at the same time we made the coconut pie, also with extra custard. Well, there were no mishaps, but the upshot was that, from the leftovers, we made a truly delicious coconut pie in a macadamia crust.

Also, as I mentioned earlier, you should keep stale cookies and crumbs because they can be used to form crusts simply by adding melted butter and egg white to the well-crumbled mixture before baking. Use the gingersnap crust on page 106 as your guide. It is a nice variation.

It is really worthwhile mastering the very simple technique of making pie crust because obviously it has so many uses. And, of course, you can also make savory pies to serve as a first course or even as the main course of a light supper.

Thickeners are often used in fruit pies so that they will be neat when sliced and so they will keep longer. However, I've never much liked the taste of thickeners and only resort to them occasionally.

Of course, custard and cream pies are a whole other story. Here, eggs are often the thickening agent and add a delicious flavor to the finished product. When making custards, be sure to stir them constantly so they won't scorch. Their flavor is so gentle that the slightest hint of scorching can be detected.

I know some people wing it and cook custards directly over the heat (and there are recipes in this chapter which tell you to do that), but if you are the least bit leery of this, cook the custard in a double boiler. Don't let the water underneath boil rapidly because this will cause curdling. And when a custard is the right thickness, continue stirring off the heat until it is fairly cool. Then, if it is to be refrigerated, press a sheet of wax paper or cling wrap directly onto the surface of the custard. This will prevent a hard film from forming as it cools.

When making meringue, add a pinch of salt or cream of tartar after egg whites have been whipped to the foamy stage. This helps to stabilize the whites once they are finished. Sugar may also be added, but if too much is used, it can reduce the meringue's volume. If you can remember to do so, always have the egg whites at room temperature when you start. When spreading finished meringue on the filling, make sure it adheres to the crust around the edges. This seals the pie and keeps the meringue from shrinking away when it is browned.

Also, humidity can have an effect on meringue. On damp or steamy days it tends to be less reliable or downright impossible.

Finally, my two favorite pies are both classics: the great all-American apple pie and the equally great lemon meringue pie.

When I first started cooking and wanted to try my hand at pie making, I naturally started with my favorite—apple pie. Like most beginners, I equated the number of ingredients with the quality of the pie, so I wasted a lot of time before discovering that, in this case, the fewer the better. Just apples, sugar, butter, and a little cinnamon. I don't know why it took me so long to figure this out. I also add grated lemon rind because I like the taste of it, but that is personal and it certainly can be left out. But no raisins, no thickeners, and nothing added to the crust.

As for lemon meringue pie, the trick was to learn how to get the crust properly baked and the custard lemony enough with the right consistency. Here my ubiquitous grated lemon rind made the difference, and I find it very necessary for a good lemon meringue pie.

So I bet if you are one of those persons who has never made a pie, you will be delighted to find out how easy it is. If you are like most people, you just have to get over your fear of making pie crusts.

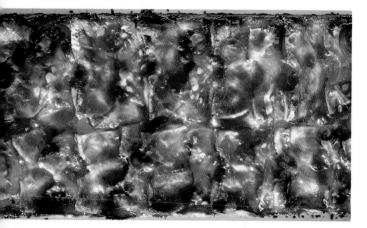

Above: Blueberry Pie
Right: Apple Pie
Below: Apple and Green
Tomato Tart

Apple Pie

The true American classic—and I don't believe in messing around with the classics. However, you could make this with a cheddar-cheese crust if you want to try a variation.

Incidentally, the pastry recipe here is from Ruth Cashdollar. She uses shortening with flecks of "meat products" in it when she comes across such a thing, which she says is often the cheaper house brand. However, I've opted for the more conventional brand.

Hot-Water Crust
1½ cups solid vegetable shortening
½ cup boiling water
2 tablespoons milk
2 teaspoons salt
    Approximately 4 cups sifted all-purpose flour

Filling
4 cups peeled, cored, and thinly sliced tart apples, such as mcintosh, granny smith, or greening (approximately 4 large apples)
1 cup sugar
¼ teaspoon salt
½ teaspoon ground cinnamon
    Finely grated rind of ½ lemon
1 tablespoon lemon juice
¼ cup (½ stick) unsalted butter, cut into bits
    Ice cream or whipped cream flavored with vanilla

To make the crust, place the shortening in a bowl and pour the boiling water over it. Stir until smooth, then add the milk. In the bowl of a food processor, fitted with the plastic blade, combine the salt and flour, then pour the shortening mixture over the flour. Process until the dough forms a mass. Form into a ball, flatten slightly between 2 sheets of wax paper, and refrigerate for at least 1 hour. This will make enough dough for two 2-crust pies. Divide the dough in half and reserve 1 half for the apple pie. I divide the other half into 2 parts and freeze both parts for later use.

Preheat the oven to 450 degrees.

Divide the reserved dough half into 2 parts, one slightly larger than the other. Roll out the larger part on a floured surface. Line a 9-inch pie pan with it and trim, leaving ½ inch around the edge. Set aside.

Place the apple slices in a large bowl. Combine the sugar, salt, and cinnamon, then mix with the apples, coating slices well. Sprinkle lemon rind and juice over all and toss. Pile into the pie pan, mounding it in the middle. Dot with the butter.

Roll out the top crust and trim to just fit. Fold the half inch excess left on the bottom crust over the top and seal by crimping edges together. Make several steam slits in the top.

Bake pie for 10 minutes, then turn oven down to 350 degrees and continue baking for an additional 30 minutes, or until the top is golden.

Serve with ice cream or slightly whipped, vanilla-flavored sweetened cream.

Serves 6 to 8

Blueberry Pie

There are two schools of thought about adding flour to the filling of a fruit pie. Obviously, it is done to thicken the juice, and there is a point to be made in favor of this. However, I prefer fruit pies made without flour. The only problem with this is that the slices don't look too great, and the pie must be served in bowls.

This recipe calls for flour, so try it that way; some other recipes (like my apple pie) don't use flour. You can make up your mind which you prefer.

Whole Wheat Short Crust
2¼ cups sifted whole wheat flour
¼ cup sugar
½ teaspoon salt
½ cup solid vegetable shortening, chilled and cut into bits
1 teaspoon distilled white vinegar
    About 6 tablespoons ice water

Filling
¼ cup all-purpose flour
⅔ cup sugar
2 teaspoons finely grated lemon zest
6 cups fresh blueberries
2 tablespoons fresh lemon juice
¼ cup (½ stick) unsalted butter, cut into bits

To make the crust, combine the whole wheat flour, sugar, and salt in the bowl of a processor fitted with the plastic dough blade. Sprinkle the shortening on top and pulse several times until the mixture resembles coarse meal.

With the motor running, add the vinegar and 2 tablespoons of the ice water. Process briefly, add 1 tablespoon more water, and pulse. Keep adding water, 1 tablespoon at the time, until the dough forms a mass.

Divide dough in half, one part slightly larger than the other. Wrap separately in plastic or wax paper and chill for at least 1 hour.

To assemble the pie, preheat the oven to 400 degrees. Combine the flour, sugar, and zest for the filling. Add the berries and toss to coat. Toss in lemon juice. Set aside.

Roll out the larger ball of dough into a 13-inch circle. Fit dough into a 10-inch pie pan, without stretching. Trim edges, leaving ½-inch overhang.

Pour the filling in and dot with butter.

Roll out the second ball of dough into a 12-inch circle. Place over filling and trim the edges. Fold over and crimp the edges. Cut 3 to 4 steam slits in the top.

Place on a foil-covered cookie sheet in the center of the oven. Bake for 20 minutes, then reduce heat to 350 and bake for an additional 25 minutes, or until browned. Let cool to room temperature on a rack.

Serves 6 to 8

Apple and Green Tomato Tart

If you have never had apples and green tomatoes combined in a pie or tart, you have a taste treat in store for you. Proceed.

- 1 cup sifted all-purpose flour
- ⅓ cup sifted confectioners' sugar
- ½ cup (1 stick) unsalted butter, softened
- 1 large tart apple or more, peeled, cored and sliced about ¼ inch thick
- 1 or 2 large green tomatoes, unpeeled, sliced ¼ inch thick
  Fresh lemon juice
- 3 tablespoons granulated sugar
- 1 tablespoon cornstarch
- ½ cup blackberry jelly, heated, or blackberry preserves, heated and sieved
  Whipped cream

Preheat the oven to 350 degrees.

Place flour, confectioners' sugar, and butter in a mixing bowl and, using your fingers, work it together to form a stiff dough. Press and pat it into the bottom of a long, thin tart pan approximately 4½ x 14 inches. It is not necessary to try to line sides. Place apple and green tomato slices, alternating and overlapping, in a single layer on top of the dough. Sprinkle generously with lemon juice. Mix sugar and cornstarch and sift over the fruit.

Bake for about 50 to 60 minutes, or until apples and tomatoes are tender, being careful not to let the crust burn. Slide the tart off onto a serving plate and pour the jelly or jam evenly over the top. Spread with your fingers, if necessary.

Serve with plain or spiked whipped cream.

Serves 6 to 8

Inset, opposite:
Coconut Cream Pie
Left: Butterscotch Pie
Above: Lemon
Meringue Pie

Butterscotch Pie

Jim Fobel's Aunt Myra makes this pie, which is unlike any other I know and tastes better than it looks. Aunt Myra deserves a medal.

Pastry
1½ cups sifted all-purpose flour
¼ teaspoon salt
½ cup solid vegetable shortening
2 to 3 tablespoons ice water

Filling
1 cup firmly packed light brown sugar
½ cup all-purpose flour
¼ teaspoon salt
1 can (13 ounces) evaporated milk
4 large egg yolks, at room temperature
¼ cup (½ stick) unsalted butter, cut into bits
1 teaspoon vanilla extract

Meringue
4 large egg whites, at room temperature
¼ teaspoon salt
¼ teaspoon cream of tartar
½ cup granulated sugar

To make the pastry, combine the flour and salt in a large bowl. Cut in the shortening until the mixture resembles coarse meal.

Sprinkle with ice water and combine with a fork. Gather dough into a ball. Place between 2 sheets of wax paper and flatten. Refrigerate for 1 hour.

Preheat the oven to 425 degrees. Roll out dough on a lightly floured surface to fit into a 9-inch pie pan and fold edges under all around the rim and crimp. Prick bottom all over with tines of a fork.

Bake crust for 12 minutes, puncturing any bubbles in the bottom of the dough that may form. The crust should be crisp and golden. Cool on a rack.

Prepare filling by combining brown sugar, flour, and salt in a bowl. Add enough water to the evaporated milk to measure 2 cups.

In another small bowl, lightly beat the egg yolks and then whisk in ½ cup of the diluted milk. Whisk the yolk mixture into the dry ingredients until thoroughly blended. Whisk in remaining diluted milk.

Transfer mixture to the top of a double boiler and cook over simmering water, whisking constantly, for 10 to 15 minutes, or until very thick. Remove from heat and stir in butter and vanilla. Cover with a round of wax paper placed directly on the surface and let cool for 15 minutes.

Pour filling into pie shell and cover again with wax paper. Let cool to room temperature and then refrigerate until well chilled, about 3 hours.

To prepare the meringue, preheat the oven to 350 degrees. Beat the egg whites with salt and cream of tartar until soft peaks form. Gradually add the sugar and continue beating until whites are stiff and glossy; do not overbeat or meringue will be dry.

Remove wax paper from filling and pile meringue on top, mounding in the center and spreading out to overlap the crust slightly all around.

Bake in the center of the oven for 12 to 15 minutes, or until meringue turns slightly golden. Chill for 3 hours before serving.

To slice, dip a sharp knife into very hot water before making each cut.

Serves 8 to 10

Lemon Meringue Pie

Jim Fobel came up with this recipe, and of all the versions I have tried and eaten over the years, this is the very best. It's hard to improve on something that is so good to begin with, but he has.

Pastry
1⅓ cups sifted all-purpose flour
½ teaspoon salt
¼ cup (½ stick) unsalted butter, chilled and cut in thin slices
¼ cup lard or solid vegetable shortening
1 teaspoon finely grated lemon zest
3 tablespoons ice water

Filling and Meringue
1½ cups superfine sugar
¼ cup plus 1 tablespoon cornstarch
½ teaspoon salt
4 large eggs, separated, at room temperature, plus 1 large egg white, at room temperature
½ cup fresh lemon juice
2 cups cold water
1½ teaspoons finely grated lemon zest
5 tablespoons unsalted butter, cut in 5 equal pieces

In a large bowl, combine the flour and salt. Cut in the butter, lard, and zest until mixture resembles coarse meal.

Sprinkle on the ice water and toss with a fork to blend. Gather dough into a ball. If excess flour remains, add a few drops more ice water. Shape into a disk and wrap in plastic. Chill for at least 1 hour.

To assemble pie, preheat oven to 425 degrees. Roll out pastry into a 12-inch circle. Fit into a 9-inch pie pan and fold edge under. Crimp.

Line the pastry shell with a sheet of foil and fill with dried beans or aluminum pie weights. Set pie pan on a baking sheet and bake for about 10 minutes, until the edge is set. Remove weights and foil. Return shell to the oven for about 5 minutes, until bottom is firm and light golden. If bottom should bubble up, tap it lightly with a spoon. Let crust cool on a rack to room temperature.

Make the filling in a large, heavy saucepan. Combine 1 cup of the sugar, the cornstarch, ¼ teaspoon salt, the 4 egg yolks, and the lemon juice. Add 2 cups cold water and whisk until blended. Cook over moderate heat, whisking constantly, until mixture comes to a boil. Boil, stirring, for 1 minute, then remove from the heat and stir in the lemon zest and butter. Stir until butter is completely melted.

Pour mixture into the pie shell, cover with a round of wax paper pressed directly on the surface, and let cool to room temperature.

Preheat the oven to 350 degrees. In a large bowl, combine the 5 egg whites and the remaining ¼ teaspoon of the salt. Beat until soft peaks form, then gradually add the remaining ½ cup sugar and beat until stiff peaks form.

Remove wax paper from top of filling and pile on meringue. Spread to slightly overlap and seal the fluted edges of the crust. (This seal is important. If the meringue does not overlap, it will shrink inward over the filling.) If desired, make decorative swirls with the back of a spoon.

Bake in the center of the oven until top is pale golden, about 10 minutes. Cool to room temperature on a rack, then refrigerate until just chilled and set, about 2 hours. Slice with a sharp knife dipped in hot water.

Serves 8 to 10

Coconut Cream Pie

If you can't find a fresh coconut or don't want to bother, use unsweetened store-bought coconut.

This recipe calls for a coconut crust, but you could, of course, use a pastry one.

Coconut Crust
2 cups shredded or grated coconut
¼ cup (½ stick) unsalted butter, melted

Filling
¼ cup cornstarch

½ cup sugar
¼ teaspoon salt
2 cups milk
⅔ cup cream of coconut
3 large egg yolks, at room temperature
1 teaspoon vanilla extract
1 tablespoon unsalted butter
1 cup shredded coconut

Meringue
3 large egg whites, at room temperature
¼ teaspoon cream of tartar
Pinch of salt
½ teaspoon vanilla extract
5 tablespoons sugar
¼ cup shredded coconut

To prepare crust, preheat oven to 325 degrees.

Combine the coconut with the melted butter. Toss with a fork until moistened, then use your hands to pat the mixture evenly into a 9-inch pie pan. Press into place so it adheres to the pan.

Bake the crust for about 20 minutes, or until golden brown and set. Let cool completely.

To make the filling, combine the cornstarch, sugar, and salt in a large saucepan. Slowly add the milk and cream of coconut, stirring constantly, over moderate heat until thickened.

In a separate bowl, whisk together the yolks and about ⅓ cup of the hot milk mixture. Stir to warm yolks, then add warmed yolks to the milk mixture and continue to cook over low heat, stirring constantly and taking care not to let custard boil, until it is thick and smooth.

Off the heat, stir in vanilla and butter, then fold in coconut. Cover with a round of wax paper pressed directly on surface of custard (keep film from forming on top), and allow to cool completely.

To bake pie, preheat oven to 325 degrees. Combine egg whites with cream of tartar, salt, and vanilla. Beat at low speed just until foamy. Increase speed and beat until whites form soft peaks. Add sugar, 1 tablespoon at a time, and beat faster until fluffy and stiff, but not hard. Do not overbeat.

Pour filling into the pie shell and smooth the top. Mound the meringue in the center and spread out to the edges, making sure meringue seals the filling completely, going all the way out to the crust.

Sprinkle the remaining coconut over the top and bake for 10 to 12 minutes, until set and browned. Let cool on a rack to room temperature. Chill for at least 2 hours before serving.

Serves 6 to 8

Above: Macadamia Cream Pie. *Below:* Impossible Pie

Above: Chess Pie. *Below:* Osgood Pie

Macadamia Cream Pie

Most nut pies have syrup-based fillings in a regular crust. However, this one is different—and the macadamia crust combined with the nutty cream mixture is delightful.

Nut Crust
1½ cups finely chopped toasted macadamia nuts*
¼ cup sugar
1 large egg white

Filling
2½ cups milk
1 vanilla bean, cut in pieces
¼ cup cornstarch
¾ cup sugar
¼ teaspoon salt
3 large egg yolks, at room temperature, lightly beaten
1 tablespoon unsalted butter
¾ cup finely chopped toasted macadamia nuts*
¾ cup coarsely chopped toasted macadamia nuts*
Whipped cream flavored with vanilla

Preheat the oven to 350 degrees.

To make the crust, lightly grease a 9-inch pie pan. Combine the nuts with the sugar. Add the egg white and stir to moisten. Pat the mixture into the pan, reaching up the sides and making as smooth a layer as possible.

Bake for 5 to 10 minutes, or until crust is set. Cool completely on a rack.

To make the filling, scald 2 cups of the milk with the vanilla bean. Set aside to steep for at least 45 minutes.

In a large saucepan, stir together the remaining ½ cup milk and the cornstarch. Add the sugar and salt. Strain the scalded milk to remove the vanilla bean, then add gradually to the milk in the saucepan, stirring over moderate heat. Stir and cook until thick, then reduce the heat to low and cook for 1 minute.

Add ⅓ cup of the mixture to the egg yolks and stir to warm them. Add the warmed yolks to the saucepan and cook for 1 to 2 minutes, just until thick and creamy. Do not allow to boil. Off the heat, stir in the butter until melted. Place the pan in a bowl of ice and beat until cooled slightly. Top with a round of wax paper and let cool to room temperature.

Stir the finely chopped nuts into the cooled cus-
tard and pour into the shell. Sprinkle coarsely chopped nuts on top and serve with flavored whipped cream.

Serves 6 to 8

* To toast the nuts, spread in a single layer on a cookie sheet with a lip. Toast in the center of a 375-degree oven for 10 minutes, stirring from time to time to prevent burning. Let cool in the pan.

Chess Pie

My Aunt Cora remembers how her grandmother, Rose Cheney Pearce, made this wonderful simple pie when she, Cora, was a child. Families were larger then, and she always made two at one time. She used a pastry crust, but here we have substituted a vanilla-wafer one.

Mrs. Pearce would then make something called "angel food pie" from the egg whites, which she would whip in a large china platter with a wire whisk, counting 100 times for each white before adding the sugar. Unfortunately, the recipe for "angel food pie" has not survived.

Vanilla-Wafer Crust
2 cups finely ground vanilla wafers
2 tablespoons sugar
Pinch of salt
½ cup (1 stick) unsalted butter, melted

Filling
6 large egg yolks
¾ cup sugar
6 tablespoons (¾ stick) unsalted butter, softened
¼ cup heavy cream

Preheat the oven to 325 degrees. Heavily butter a 9-inch pie pan. Set aside.

Toss the wafer crumbs with the sugar and salt. Add the melted butter and toss again with a fork to moisten. Press mixture into the pie pan, lining the bottom and sides and making it as smooth as possible. Place pan on a cookie sheet in the center of the oven and bake for 10 minutes, or until set. Allow to cool on a rack.

Turn oven up to 350 degrees. Beat the yolks, sugar, and softened butter together until smooth, then beat in the cream. Pour mixture into the pie crust and bake for about 30 minutes, or until golden brown and set. Watch carefully to make sure it doesn't overcook.

Serves 6 to 8

Impossible Pie

I suppose this recipe gets its name from the fact that all the ingredients are dropped into a food processor (or blender) and whirled around, then poured into a pie pan and baked—making it seem unlikely that anything good could come from such a mess. But the mixture magically makes its own crustlike bottom and is very tasty. Anyway, it couldn't be easier.

- 1 cup sugar
- 4 large eggs
- 2 cups milk
- ½ cup (1 stick) unsalted butter or margarine, melted
- ½ cup sifted all-purpose flour
- 1 teaspoon vanilla extract
- 1 cup fresh flaked coconut
- ½ cup honey-roasted peanuts
  Bourbon Whipped Cream (page 150)

Preheat the oven to 350 degrees.

Combine all the ingredients in the bowl of a food processor and process for 1 minute. Pour mixture into a 10-inch pie pan.

Bake for 1 hour or until set. Serve with spiked whipped cream.

Serves 8

Osgood Pie

Osgood pie is a relative of mince pie, but better. This one goes over big.

- 1 recipe Sweet Crust (page 102)
- 3 tablespoons all-purpose flour
- 1 cup golden raisins
- 1 cup coarsely chopped pecans or pecan pieces
- 6 tablespoons (¾ stick) unsalted butter, softened
- ¾ cup firmly packed light brown sugar
- 3 large eggs, separated, at room temperature
- 2 tablespoons sour-mash whiskey, such as Jack Daniel's
- 1 teaspoon distilled white vinegar
- 1 teaspoon ground cinnamon
- ½ teaspoon freshly grated nutmeg
- ½ teaspoon ground allspice
  Pinch of salt
- 1 cup heavy cream, whipped with 2 teaspoons sour-mash whiskey and 2 tablespoons sugar

Preheat the oven to 350 degrees. Roll out the crust and fit into a 9-inch pie pan. Place pan on a cookie sheet and set aside.

Toss the flour, raisins, and pecans in a bowl to coat well. Set aside.

Cream the butter and brown sugar until smooth, about 3 minutes. Add the egg yolks, 1 at the time, beating after each addition. Add the whiskey, vinegar, cinnamon, nutmeg, and allspice. Mix well, then add the floured nut-and-raisin mixture.

Beat the egg whites with the salt until stiff. Gently fold whites into the nut mixture.

Mound filling into the pie crust and smooth the top. Bake in the center of the oven for 25 to 30 minutes, or until puffed and set.

Serve warm or at room temperature, topped with a dollop of spiked whipped cream.

Serves 6 to 8

Left: Strawberry Pie;
Rhubarb Pie
Above: Chocolate Cream
_Pie with Chocolate
Meringue_

Strawberry Pie

Strawberry pie is an invention of the same Mary Allen who sent me the rhubarb pie recipe. Actually, you can use the basic recipe to make blackberry, blueberry, or raspberry pies; just adjust the amount of sugar.

You can use any crust. The one here is sweetened.

Sweet Crust
1½ cups sifted all-purpose flour
¾ teaspoon salt
2 tablespoons sugar
5 tablespoons ice water
¼ cup solid vegetable shortening, chilled
2 tablespoons (¼ stick) unsalted butter, chilled, cut into bits

Filling
Approximately 1½ quarts fresh berries
1 cup sugar
3 tablespoons cornstarch
½ cup water
1 tablespoon unsalted butter
1 cup heavy cream, whipped and flavored with 1 teaspoon vanilla extract

To make the crust, sift together the flour, salt, and sugar. Remove ⅓ cup of this, place in a small bowl, and add the ice water. Stir to make a paste, and set aside.

Add the shortening and butter to the balance of the flour and cut in with 2 knives or a pastry blender (this may also be done in a food processor). Combine with the paste, and mix until dough can be shaped into a ball. Place ball of dough between 2 sheets of wax paper and flatten slightly. Refrigerate for 30 minutes.

Preheat the oven to 425 degrees.

Roll out the dough on a lightly floured surface. Place in a 9-inch pie pan, and trim, leaving ½ inch all around. Fold edge under and then crimp. Place a sheet of foil on top of the pastry and weight it down with dried beans. Bake for 5 to 7 minutes, or until edges begin to firm. Remove foil and beans, and continue baking for another 10 minutes, or until golden brown. Carefully loosen edges. When almost cool, slide off onto a serving plate. Set aside.

Mash enough berries to fill 1 cup. Cut balance in half, saving a few perfect ones for a garnish.

Combine the crushed berries, sugar, cornstarch, and water in a small saucepan and cook over medium heat, stirring constantly, until mixture comes to a boil. Continue cooking for about 2 minutes over low heat until mixture is thickened and clear. Stir in the butter and cook until melted, then allow to cool slightly.

Place the halved berries in the baked crust and pour the cooked ones over them. Shake the serving plate gently so the glaze seeps down around the raw berries.

Chill for a few hours, then serve topped with the flavored whipped cream.

Serves 6 to 8

Rhubarb Pie

When she sent this recipe, Mary Allen, whom I met about ten years ago in Connecticut, wrote me that it was given to her by a woman who had died four years before at the age of eighty-eight. Mary went on to say that the woman had gone to work at the age of only sixteen as a "hired girl" in a Roxbury, Connecticut, home where she continued to work for the rest of her long life. This was the favorite pie in that household. I'm pleased it comes with such sterling credentials, because I must confess that rhubarb is not a favorite of mine. However, all rhubarb fanciers who tried it pronounced it first rate.

Short Crust
2 cups sifted all-purpose flour
2 tablespoons sugar
¼ teaspoon salt
½ cup (1 stick) unsalted butter, chilled and cut into 8 pieces
1 large egg yolk
2 to 3 tablespoons ice water

Filling
4½ cups chopped fresh rhubarb, in ¾- to 1-inch lengths
1¼ cups sugar
3 tablespoons honey
¼ teaspoon salt
3 tablespoons fresh lemon juice or orange juice
2 tablespoons (¼ stick) unsalted butter, melted
6 tablespoons all-purpose flour

To make the crust, place the flour, sugar, and salt in the bowl of a food processor fitted with a plastic dough blade. Sprinkle the butter pieces over the top and add the egg yolk. Pulse, turning machine on and off, until mixture resembles coarse grain.

With motor on, add 2 tablespoons of the ice water and process just until the dough masses together into a ball (add the other tablespoon of water if needed). Remove dough from processor and knead in any remaining flour.

Divide dough in 2 parts, one slightly larger than the other. Wrap separately in plastic and refrigerate for at least 1 hour.

To assemble the pie, preheat the oven to 350 degrees. Mix the filling ingredients in a bowl. Toss to coat the rhubarb and set aside.

Roll out the larger piece of dough and line a 9-inch pan. Do this gently, because this dough does not stretch very well (it breaks, instead). Trim, leaving ½ inch overhang. Pour filling in and refrigerate while you make the lattice crust.

Roll out other piece of dough and cut into ½- to ¾-inch strips (a rolling pizza cutter is good for this). Weave the strips of dough into a lattice crust on the filled pie. Fold the overhanging pastry edge up to enclose the strips of lattice and crimp to seal well.

Place pan on a cookie sheet covered with foil and bake in the center of the oven for 45 to 50 minutes or until the crust is golden and the rhubarb can be pierced easily with a fork. Let cool on a rack.

Serves 6 to 8

Chocolate Cream Pie with Chocolate Meringue

This is pretty sweet for a chocolate pie, but also pretty darn good. You could forego the meringue, but that is part of the fun.

Crust
1 cup sifted all-purpose flour
½ teaspoon salt
6 tablespoons solid vegetable shortening, chilled and cut into bits
2 to 3 tablespoons ice water

Filling
3 large egg yolks, at room temperature
¾ cup sugar
¼ cup cornstarch
½ teaspoon salt
2 cups buttermilk

3 ounces unsweetened chocolate, melted
2 tablespoons (¼ stick) unsalted butter
1 teaspoon vanilla extract

Meringue
4 large egg whites, at room temperature
½ teaspoon cream of tartar
Pinch of salt
6 tablespoons sugar
1 ounce unsweetened chocolate, melted and cooled to room temperature

Combine the flour and salt in the bowl of a food processor fitted with a plastic blade. Sprinkle shortening on top and process until grainy. With machine running, add 2 tablespoons of ice water and process until dough masses together. Add the additional tablespoon of water if needed.

Gather the dough into a ball and flatten between 2 sheets of wax paper. Refrigerate for at least 1 hour.

Preheat the oven to 350 degrees.

Roll the dough out onto a lightly floured surface into a 12-inch circle. Line a 9-inch pie pan with it and trim the edges leaving ½ inch of the crust to fold under and crimp. Line crust with a sheet of foil and fill with dried beans or aluminum pie weights. Place on a baking sheet and bake for 10 minutes. Remove foil and beans. Continue to bake for an additional 5 to 8 minutes, or until golden. Cool on a wire rack.

Meanwhile, to make the filling, beat the yolks and place them in a large nonstick saucepan. Stir in the sugar, cornstarch, salt, and buttermilk. Cook over moderate heat, stirring constantly, until very thick and mixture stirs into fairly stiff mounds.

Off the heat, stir in the melted chocolate. Add the butter and vanilla, stirring until butter melts completely. Place a round of wax paper directly on the surface of the chocolate cream and chill.

To assemble the pie, preheat the oven to 400 degrees. Mound the filling in the crust and smooth the top. Beat the egg whites, cream of tartar, and pinch of salt until foamy, then add sugar, 1 tablespoon at a time. At the lowest speed, fold in the melted chocolate. Work quickly and gently so meringue does not deflate too much.

Mound meringue on top of filling and smooth out to sides, sealing it to the edges of the crust (this is important). Bake for 5 to 10 minutes—just until meringue is lightly browned. Let cool on a rack to room temperature. Chill thoroughly before serving cold.

Serves 6 to 8

Above: Sugar Tart. *Below:* Pear Tarts.

Above: Pumpkin Chiffon Pie. *Below:* Walnut Tart

Sugar Tart

Cookbook author, teacher, and chef Evelyne Slomon makes this marvelous tart that's filled very simply with cooked-down heavy cream. You have to taste it to understand it—it is absolutely delicious. This recipe, which is based on an old French country-style tart, was inspired by three-star chef Freddy Girardet's recipe for tarte vaudoise.

½ cup (1 stick) unsalted butter, chilled and cut into bits
⅓ cup plus 1 tablespoon milk
⅓ cup plus 6 tablespoons sugar
¼ teaspoon salt
2⅔ cups sifted all-purpose flour
1½ teaspoons baking powder
1⅓ cups heavy cream
    Ground cinnamon
1½ cups washed fresh raspberries, blackberries, or sliced strawberries; or a combination of the 3
    Sugar
¼ cup Grand Marnier, kirsch, or framboise

Garnish
Mint leaves

Preheat the oven to 425 degrees. Generously butter a 9-inch loose-bottom tart pan. Set aside.

In a processor fitted with the plastic blade, combine butter, ⅓ cup milk, ⅓ cup sugar, and the salt. Process for a few seconds, just until blended.

Sift together the flour and baking powder, then add to the butter mixture. Process until lumps begin to form. If necessary, add the remaining tablespoon milk.

Gather the dough into a ball and roll out on a floured board into a 10-inch circle. Fit dough into prepared pan without stretching. Fold edge over tart and crimp. Be careful not to have any thin areas in the dough, or the filling will run underneath. Sprinkle the remaining 6 tablespoons of sugar over the bottom of the tart shell.

Place pan on a baking sheet and put on the middle rack of the oven. Carefully pour the cream over the sugar, and sprinkle on cinnamon to taste—don't overdo.

Bake the tart for 10 minutes, then reduce the heat to 400 degrees and continue baking until cream is browned, bubbly, and moves only slightly when pan is jiggled. If large bubbles form during baking, pierce carefully with a knife. Take care not to puncture crust. Allow tart to cool on a rack.

Marinate the berries with sugar to taste in the liqueur for about 1 hour. Reheat the tart in a 200-degree oven and serve warm, napped with some of the fruit. If desired, garnish with mint leaves.

Serves 6 to 8

Pumpkin Chiffon Pie

There is one secret to this marvelous spicy pie with its gingersnap crust: Avoid refrigerating it because if you do, the crust will get cold and harden. So make and bake the crust and set it aside. (Or, if you must refrigerate it, allow it to come back to room temperature before going on with the recipe.) Prepare the filling and refrigerate it. Then assemble the whole thing, which takes only minutes, just before you want to serve the pie.

Gingersnap Crust
2 cups finely crushed gingersnap cookies
2 to 3 tablespoons sugar (depending on the sweetness of the cookies)
    Pinch of salt
½ cup (1 stick) unsalted butter, melted

Filling and Topping
1 envelope unflavored gelatin
1 cup evaporated milk
2 cups solid-pack canned pumpkin
¾ cup firmly packed light brown sugar
    Pinch of salt
2 large eggs, separated, at room temperature
1 teaspoon ground cinnamon
½ teaspoon freshly grated nutmeg
½ teaspoon ground allspice
½ teaspoon ground ginger
¼ teaspoon ground cloves
3 tablespoons granulated sugar
1 cup heavy cream, whipped

Preheat the oven to 325 degrees. Very heavily butter a 9-inch pie pan. Set aside.

Combine the crumbs, sugar, and salt in a bowl. Pour in the melted butter, and toss with a fork until crumbs are moistened. Press mixture evenly into the buttered pie pan. Place pan on a baking sheet and bake for 10 minutes. Cool completely on a rack before filling.

Whisk the gelatin into the evaporated milk and set aside to soften.

In a large saucepan (nonstick, if possible), combine pumpkin, brown sugar, and salt. Place over moderate heat and cook until warmed through. Add the milk mixture and cook, stirring constantly, until the mixture comes to a boil. Remove from the heat and set aside.

Beat the yolks in a small bowl. Add about ⅓ cup of the pumpkin mixture and stir to warm the yolks. Then add the yolks to the saucepan and stir over moderately low heat until well blended. Add the spices and cook, stirring, until very thick, about 2 to 3 minutes.

Place a round of wax paper directly on the surface and let cool to room temperature.

Beat the egg whites to soft peaks. Add the granulated sugar and continue to beat until stiff. Fold the whites into the pumpkin mixture only just until no white streaks show. Top with a round of wax paper and refrigerate until well chilled.

To serve, mound the filling into the crust and smooth the top. Pile the whipped cream on top and serve at once.

Serves 6 to 8

Walnut Tart

Walnut tart is a relative of pecan pie, but the walnuts give a completely different flavor. You could use any short pie crust, but I think the one for the pear tart works well. Roll it out rather thicker than you would for the pear tart.

- 1 recipe for Pear Tart Crust (recipe follows)
- 1½ cups coarsely chopped walnuts
- 1 cup sugar
- 1 tablespoon all-purpose flour
- 3 large eggs
- 1 cup light corn syrup
- 2 tablespoons (¼ stick) butter, melted
- 1 tablespoon dark rum, or 1 teaspoon vanilla extract
  Cream or ice cream

Preheat the oven to 375 degrees.

Line an 8 x 8-inch glass baking pan with the dough, allowing any excess to drape over the sides. Sprinkle the walnuts evenly over the bottom. Set aside.

Mix the sugar and flour, then beat in the eggs until well mixed. Add the corn syrup and melted butter, then stir in the rum and mix thoroughly. Pour mixture over the walnuts. Bring dough up around sides to flop over filling.

Bake for 50 to 60 minutes, or until puffed and firmed. Serve with ice cream or plain cream.

Serves 8

Pear Tart

I have used raspberry jelly to glaze this tart because I like the combination of the two flavors of pear and raspberry. You might experiment with other jams, if you like.

Crust
- ¾ cup solid vegetable shortening
- ¼ cup boiling water
- 1 teaspoon salt
- 1 tablespoon milk
  Approximately 2 cups sifted all-purpose flour

Filling
- 6 small pears, peeled, cored, and sliced thin
  Fresh lemon juice
- 3 tablespoons sugar
- 1 tablespoon cornstarch
- ¼ teaspoon grated nutmeg
- ⅛ teaspoon finely ground black pepper
- ½ cup raspberry jelly, heated, or raspberry preserves, heated and sieved
  Whipped cream flavored with pear brandy

To make the crust, place shortening in a large bowl and pour the boiling water over. Stir to melt and make a smooth mixture. Add the salt and milk, and stir to mix. Add the flour, ½ cup at the time, mixing well after each addition until you have added 1½ cups. After that, add flour just until the mixture clings together and makes a stiff dough. Form into a ball, flatten between 2 sheets of wax paper, and refrigerate for at least 1 hour.

Preheat the oven to 350 degrees.

Roll out dough on a floured surface. Line a long, thin tart pan approximately 4½ x 14 inches. Slightly separate the pear slices and lay each pear on the dough crosswise (or in an even pattern) in the pan. Sprinkle lemon juice over. Combine the sugar, cornstarch, nutmeg, and pepper, and sift over the pears.

Bake for 50 minutes, or until pears are tender. While still hot, loosen the edges and slide the tart onto a serving platter. Pour the melted jelly or preserves over the top and smooth out, with fingers if necessary.

Serve with flavored whipped cream.

Serves 6

Apples

Apricots

Bananas

Blackberries

Blueberries

Cherries

Figs

Grapes

Grapefruit

Kiwifruit

Mangos

Melons

Oranges

Peaches

Pears

Pineapple

Plums

Raspberries

Strawberries

Fresh Fruit

Previous page: Poached Fruit

Fresh fruit just can't be beat as a light and refreshing way to end a meal. Dessert may be as plain as a basket of figs or as elaborate as a glistening crystal bowl of peaches and berries chilling in champagne. Either way (and many ways in between) you and your guests are guaranteed a satisfying finish. And visually, fruit has almost no peers.

Unfortunately, growers have had more success with making fresh fruit look good year round than they have had with making it taste as good as it looks. This is why I generally eat uncooked fruit only in season. The exceptions are the old standbys of apples, pears, and bananas.

As a category, fruit is remarkably versatile. Think of the things you can make with pears, for instance. If you poach them in wine, you get one thing; if you poach them in simple syrup and peppercorns, quite another. Of course, pears may be used to make end-less elegant tarts and all sorts of ices, ice creams, and flavorings for custards and pudding. And served with an assortment of cheese, pears can hold their own against any other dessert.

Of the various fruits listed here, almost all can be used in one or more of the ways that pears can. And when you have had enough of one particular fruit, you can start all over and combine it with an assort-ment of others, creating even greater variety.

Even if you have only the smallest sunny plot, you can still grow at least one kind of fruit. And on an apartment terrace you can grow strawberries in tubs or barrels. I have peach trees, raspberry canes, and wild strawberry plants at my house in Bridge-hampton, Long Island. When these bear, I have not only all the peaches and berries to satisfy my taste for them, but enough to enjoy passing around to friends.

So if you have to concentrate on one category of desserts, this is for you. A feast for the senses—and healthful, too.

That said, I hope you don't confine yourself to just one group of desserts, but go on to find the taste treats in store for you in those sinful cookies, melt-ing custards, and the like.

I selected the fruits we photographed for these pages at random, ignoring melons, pineapples, bananas, citrus, and probably more. We had limited space for photographs, and I simply chose what looked best in the market on the day we did the pictures.

Some of the ways I suggest serving the fruits that we *did* photograph can easily be applied to other, not featured, fruits. This is just to get you going.

Apples

Apples probably are the most flexible and most reliable fruit, from a flavor standpoint, of all the readily available fruits. They are at their best in the fall and through late March, but they store so well that you don't have to worry too much about their having flavor. This year-round availability doesn't apply to all varieties, so eat the rarer and special favorites in season.

Apples may be used in all sorts of tarts and pies, as well as to make sauces to serve as desserts (and with meats). I especially like apples cored, peeled, cut into large pieces, sprinkled with brown sugar, and sautéed in butter. Or try coring apples and stuffing their centers with blue or some other kind of cheese to take on picnics.

Once raw apples have been halved or peeled, give them a rubbing of lemon juice, or some other citrus juice, to keep them from turning dark.

Incidentally, dessert apple sauce blends very nicely with other stewed fruits, such as blueberries.

Apricots

My favorite way to eat an apricot is poached in simple syrup, with the addition of a spice like cinnamon or cloves. Don't go overboard on the spices.

Unlike apples, apricots should really only be eaten in season, roughly from mid-May to mid-August.

Bananas

Another of the most reliable of the year-round fruits, bananas are best bought fairly green and allowed to ripen at home. This can take a day or two. I don't like my bananas overly ripe.

Being from Louisiana, I have had my share of baked and sautéed bananas. The only drawback is that such desserts cannot be prepared too far in advance. But if you are handy with a chafing dish, you can sauté bananas at the table. I'd try this on the family, however, before tackling it for a party.

I know we are told not to keep bananas in the refrigerator, but nobody said not to keep them in the freezer. Frozen bananas can be puréed in a food processor and topped with a little fruit syrup. It's a marvelous low-sugar dessert.

Try serving bananas uncooked, sliced and drizzled with pineapple juice and a sprinkling of coarse brown sugar. Garnish with orange sections.

Cherries

Cherries have a season that is about the same as the apricot's and, like apricots, are best eaten right at their peak. I like them best of all raw, served in a bowl of ice and water. They are marvelous for serving after a summer lunch under a shady awning. And, of course, if you are going to cook them, there is the classic summer favorite, the clafouti.

Incidentally, if you like clafouti, try making it with bananas, too.

Figs

I think my favorite way of eating fresh figs is to poach them lightly in simple syrup with a few strips of lemon rind and a piece of ginger. This may be enhanced with a bit of flavored cream.

For purists, nothing can beat plain fresh figs, eaten skin and all.

Clockwise from above:
Apples; Red Grapes; Red Plums; Plums; Kiwi

Top: Peaches
Above: Pears
Right: Figs

Grapes

I love frozen grapes. That way, they become a delicious light snack or refreshing luncheon dessert. There is nothing to it; just pull seedless grapes from the stems and lay them out on a piece of wax paper in the freezer.

As you know, grapes are pretty widely available year round, but there are a few varieties, such as the small brown champagne grape, which only turn up at the end of the summer. They are worth waiting for and worth looking for.

Pears

Pears are an extremely versatile fruit and, because of their stable texture when poached, they also make a marvelously attractive presentation. I especially like pears poached in strong, heavily sweetened coffee or wine syrup. Not only do these liquids give pears a delicious flavor, but they dye them a beautiful color.

Not to be overlooked, of course, is the classic pears and cheese for dessert. Beautiful simplicity.

You can have good, fresh pears almost all year long just by following the various varieties as they come into season. Go from bartletts to kiefers on to comices, anjous, boscs, and nelis.

Pears should be bought hard and allowed to ripen at home. A piece of tree-ripened fruit wouldn't last until it got to the market, so pears are picked green. The ripening happens very quickly, so a pear bought firm one day is perfect the following evening for dinner.

The flavor of poached pears is complemented by pepper and also by chocolate. And do make pear ice, page 11, which is one of my favorites.

Mangos

Of course, mangos make a very interesting-tasting chutney, but I think they are at their very best eaten raw with a squeeze of lemon or lime.

The important thing to remember about mangos is that they really should be chilled before eating. And they look very pretty served in a bowl of cracked ice.

Store them in the refrigerator, wrapped loosely.

Oranges

The best of all the dessert oranges are the blood oranges from Spain and Italy. Not only do they have a lovely flavor, but their flesh is flecked with all shades of color, ranging from the usual orange all the way through pink to reddish purple. Simply peel them, scraping away as much of the white pith as possible, then slice thickly and sprinkle with sugar. Perfect and perfectly beautiful. They are best chilled.

Regular sliced oranges can be dressed with brown sugar and dusted with a little cinnamon. Or they may be enhanced with a sprinkling of toasted coconut.

And finally, oranges are part of one of my favorite old desserts: ambrosia. This can be as simple as tossed orange sections and grated coconut or as complicated as the deluxe versions that include bananas, pineapple, marshmallows, and grapes, For me, less is more here, so I opt for the orange and coconut combination. Grand Marnier is also sometimes added, but it seems out of place to me. Always serve ambrosia chilled, and don't make it too far in advance because it will start to ferment.

Kiwifruit

For a while, right after nouvelle cuisine first hit the scene, it seemed as if we were being "kiwied" to death. That's too bad, because kiwi (also called Chinese gooseberry, incidentally) is a delicious fruit, with a flavor that seems to combine several other familiar ones. And it is very decorative. Serve it peeled, sliced, and with a little citrus juice sprinkled over all. If kiwi are really in season and ripe, they don't need sugar.

Grapefruit

Grapefruit sorbet or sherbet is just about the best way of eating grapefruit, for my money. I like it with crystallized grapefruit rind and a sprig of mint.

When preparing raw grapefruit, after it is peeled, a very quick submersion in boiling water (only a few seconds) will make peeling off any remaining white pith easier.

Plums

Plums make very good tarts, which is how I most often serve them, but you can poach them in simple syrup with the addition of a spice or two.

Plums are pretty messy to eat raw, so they are best served in an outdoor or informal setting.

Melons

This fairly large and diverse group includes:

Cantaloupes, at their best during the summer season when they are sweetest.

Casabas, which are available all the way up to the end of December.

Crenshaws, which are good from early summer up into the early fall.

Honeydews, which are available almost all year long, but are best eaten in their real season, July through September.

Persians, similar to cantaloupe, with a season like the honeydews.

Watermelons, a childhood favorite of most everyone, and should be eaten in summer only.

Interestingly enough, cantaloupe seems to make the best sherbet, and watermelon the least good.

Melons can be cut in balls and mixed with other fruit or served by the wedge. Always include a slice of lemon or lime with raw melon and a sprig of sugared mint if it is handy.

Peaches

When I was growing up peaches were my favorite fruit. Peach cobbler, peach ice cream, or peaches right off the tree, skin and all. You just couldn't beat it, as far as I was concerned. Then when I was in my twenties, I lived in Italy for about six months and was so broke I had to live on peaches and pasta for the last half of my stay. This ruined my taste for them for years. Luckily, things are right again.

When they are really ripe, peaches need only be peeled and sliced, with a sprinkling of sugar and a slick of cream to create a perfect dessert. The sugar may be granulated, confectioners', or brown; yogurt, sour cream, or crème fraîche can be substituted for regular cream.

Peaches, like apples and pears, should be rubbed lightly with lemon juice to keep them from turning dark.

And finally, although I say that blackberry cobbler is my favorite, peach cobbler is not far behind.

Pineapple

The least difficult and most decorative way of serving fresh pineapple is to cut a whole one in half and carve out the flesh, leaving the skin as a boat container to heap the cubed flesh back into. If pineapple is really ripe, and there is no point in buying any other kind, it will require no sugar. You can also freeze these chunks before piling them back into the skin.

Pineapple also combines very well with other fresh fruit, especially berries and melon. Always be sure to cut out the eyes when you peel and cube it.

The top of a pineapple will continue to stay green and grow slightly if placed on a sunny window sill in a saucer containing a little water.

Above: Blueberries. *Below:* Raspberries

Above: Strawberries. *Below:* Blackberries

Blackberries

Blackberries always tend to be a bit more tart than other berries, so they usually need some sort of sweetener. Although often available during the year, like almost everything else, blackberries are best whey they have had a chance to mature and ripen on the cane. Their season is roughly from May to the middle of August, depending on where you are. But their peak is generally at the beginning to middle of summer.

Try blackberries sweetened with a little sugar and bathed in flavored cream, either whipped or not. Because they are so tart, I don't think they blend as well with yogurt, crème fraîche, and sour cream as do other berries.

Whole blackberries may be combined with other puréed fruits, such as peaches or pears. When you do this, add just a few drops of lemon juice to the purée to keep it from turning dark. Their flavor may also be enhanced by soaking the berries in a little blackberry liqueur or some other spirit.

Unfortunately, freezing destroys the texture of blackberries, but luckily not their flavor. In a pinch you might make a purée of frozen berries to top melon balls or as the basis for a frozen dessert. For the frozen dessert, simply purée the berries with a little sugar to taste and a drop of liqueur; strain the pulp and freeze it as you would any other sherbet. Tasty and light.

Or you might make one of those composed desserts using blackberries along with other fresh fruit and topping it with a fruit purée. For example, place slices of fresh pineapple and some melon on individual serving plates. Add to this a purée of fresh or frozen berries and peeled fresh plums (it won't take too many plums, so peeling them will not be too tedious), to which you have added a squeeze of orange juice (make sure everything is fresh, if you can) and a grating of nutmeg—and some kind of sweetener, if needed. Sprinkle blackberries over this, and grate a bit of lemon rind on the whole dish.

Neatness counts here, as you are not only creating a delicious-tasting dessert but one which should be a visual treat.

Strawberries

Today, strawberries are available in some quantity all year round. Unfortunately, though not as poor as the out-of-season tomatoes we have to put up with, they often look a lot better than they taste. Those overly large berries with stems attached that you see in the fancy markets cost an arm and a leg and are apt to be almost hollow in the middle. So if you are in it for taste, wait until the season, when you can really enjoy their marvelous flavor.

In the meantime, strawberry flavor seems to survive freezing pretty well. If you have the space in your freezing compartment, you might want to make a simple strawberry purée when they are plentiful—in season—to enjoy later.

Puréed berries are much more compact than whole or sliced ones, and since freezing is going to ruin their texture anyway, there is no use taking up the room in your freezer to store whole berries.

And, of course, when strawberries are really at their most succulent, usually from April through June, you should indulge yourself at least once and make a wonderful strawberry shortcake, still one of the best desserts going. I like my strawberries on sweet biscuits that are served buttered and warm, if I can swing it. Failing that, use any sort of not-too-sweet cake topped with berries that have been mashed with a little sugar and allowed to sit in the refrigerator for about 15 or 20 minutes. Top this with a generous spoonful of whipped cream and a few freshly halved and sugared berries.

I only tried to grow domestic strawberries once, and I gave up because they required too much care and weeding, and because their runners spread new plants faster than I could keep up with them. However, I have never tried a strawberry barrel but have always thought that might be a good idea once you got the hang of it. At least you would get enough berries for your breakfast cereal.

What do grow remarkably well, and with little care required, are fraises des bois, which are, literally, "woods' strawberries" or wild strawberries. They bloom and set fruit continually and don't move around the way domestic ones do. Their only drawback is that these wild berries are, as you would imagine, smaller and not as sweet.

Incidentally, my favorite way to eat strawberries is how they are often prepared in Italy—with sugar and a squeeze of lemon juice, and nothing else. The berries should be cut in half and allowed to marinate for about half an hour before serving. It's just about as good as they can get.

Blueberries

I hadn't tasted blueberries until I was a teenager, since they don't grow where I was brought up. And my childhood was past before the more perishable fruits and vegetables were shipped regularly all over the country. So the truth is, I simply don't think of them as much as I do strawberries and blackberries, which I grew up with.

One of my favorite ways to eat fresh blueberries is with crème fraîche and a little brown sugar sprinkled over them, topped with a grating of lemon rind. Blueberries are usually sweet enough naturally not to need much help in that department—the brown sugar is more for flavor variety. And they are also sweet enough to balance the slightly sour quality of the crème fraîche.

Of course, you might want to do up blueberries with flavored cream, but I really also think the berries lend themselves nicely to being dressed with a few generous spoonfuls of cold vanilla-custard sauce.

Fairly good blueberries are now available (from Nova Scotia, I understand) all the way up to the end of September and slightly beyond. That means they can be mixed with fall raspberries to make a marvelously sensual fresh dessert. Add a little thick cream to the mix, and you are in heaven.

If you are ambitious, you might want to use fresh berries combined with crêpes and topped with confectioners' sugar. I'm not much for doing such complicated desserts after dinner; however I think such a concoction would be fun to serve on a Sunday afternoon in the country, just before everyone gets ready to leave for the city.

Incidentally, blueberry bushes are very neat and easy to grow, so if you have the space you might want to give them a try. They thrive very happily wherever the soil is fairly good and the weather is cool. They also grow wild, but gathering wild blueberries is really a time-consuming affair. Also, the plump domestic berries sold in the stores are several times larger than their wild relative.

Blueberries apparently freeze better than most, but I still would rather use the frozen ones only puréed into a sauce as part of a dessert. As a matter of fact, blueberry purée makes store-bought cake and ice cream, with the addition of a little whipped cream or some other cream, into a delightful, triflelike treat.

Raspberries

The first thing that most people say about raspberries is that they are expensive—and that's true. This is because they are so fragile and must be picked ripe to be sold quickly before starting to go bad. For that reason, of all the common berries, ever-bearing raspberries are the ones you should go to the trouble to cultivate. And for your trouble, you get two crops from your canes: one at the beginning of the summer and another in the fall. In my locale, the raspberry seasons are in June and at the end of September. As a matter of fact, raspberries are so easily grown that if you plant a couple dozen canes you will be giving berries away or making everything you can think of from them when they ripen. Just plant your raspberries where they can have room, as they tend to spread rapidly and don't look too neat.

Of course, if you find yourself driving in the country up in Vermont or New Hampshire, keep an eye out along the back roads, where you are likely to find great quantities of wild berries. They are fairly large, and, although pretty thorny, not too time-consuming to gather.

I especially like making raspberry syrup from my berries, when I have had my fill of them with cream and sugar. This syrup comes in handy as a topping, and may be thinned with a little water to make a very good quick ice.

Raspberries don't make especially good cobblers because they don't have quite enough body, but as you will see on page 83, I have combined them with pears in a cobbler. The two flavors complement each other very nicely.

And something else about raspberries that I like is their marvelous color. Whenever you make cold (or hot, which I never undertake) soufflés or mousses, their juice stains them to a lovely dark pink.

However, as pretty as it is, I don't care much for raspberry ice cream. Raspberries are really better as an ice or as a very light sherbet.

For a change, you might want to try a raspberry shortcake, made just like a strawberry shortcake.

Finally, as with the other berries just mentioned, raspberries can be utilized frozen to make purées and toppings.

And if you are in the mood for a beautiful and potent drink, try filling a bottle with fresh raspberries and then drowning the whole thing with vodka. Put it in the freezer to age a few days and serve neat, if you dare, or with tonic water.

Cookies

Cookies make me think of grandmothers, summer, ice cream, lemonade, and sand tarts made with real sand.

About the *real sand* tarts—you know how literal children are. Well, I was no exception. Sand tarts were my first attempt at making cookies. I wasn't that interested in cooking, but I was really interested in cookies, so I figured that if I could learn to make them myself, I would avoid several middlemen (or middlewomen). Anyway, I got our cook to show me what went into sand tarts. As you might know, the ingredients are simplicity itself: butter, flour, sugar, and ground nuts. It was the ground nuts that fouled me up. You see, this all took place in the dark days before there was a Cuisinart or any other magic electric nut-grinding machine (I wouldn't have been allowed to touch it, if there had been one). So this meant grating nuts by hand—in my case, grating my knuckles as well. I naively thought that, since the nuts were in the cookies to approximate the texture of sand and since grinding nuts was more than I bargained for, . . . well, you know the rest. It wasn't easy being green. And in this case, it could actually have been unhealthful if my eagle-eyed mother hadn't caught me.

In those days, I think my grandmother actually smelled like a cookie. That's enough to get any child's attention. And hanging around her as she cooked was a pleasant change from dealing with my mother, who never learned to cook anyway. As for lemonade and ice cream, everyone knows that cookies with either is a marriage made in heaven.

It is interesting how much the public's taste in cookies has changed since the late thirties, when I was a child. Then, almost all cookies were crisp, with modest but intense flavors. They were filled with nuts and raisins at times, of course, but they were not really big productions the way they often are now. And the cookies were mostly rather small. They could almost have been made while you were doing something else. It also seems they were always made in gigantic quantities, which meant that they must have lasted quite well, with those like shortbread and tea cakes improving with age.

Often, cookies were served in the afternoon with something else as a little treat (or as a bribe to quiet children). Today's cookies are almost a meal in themselves. And they certainly dominate anything you have with them, so they are best with the simplest of drinks. Luckily, I like both today's and yesterday's versions. But people who haven't tasted the flavor of an unassuming crisp little cookie have missed something very nice indeed. There are examples here of those small treats, like the cracked sugar cookies on page 127.

Although I have always made cookies from time to time, until I got going on this book I never fully realized how much of a difference changing the proportions of a few quite ordinary ingredients can make. A little more of this and a little less of that and you have a completely different cookie. Leave out a spice or add grated lemon rind instead of vanilla, and you are on your way to inventing your own cookie. And with more complicated items like brownies, the sky is the limit. So don't be shy about tailoring a recipe to make it more to your liking after you have given it a try and understand it.

When baking cookies I use a double-walled baking sheet (see page 163) because it makes them brown more evenly. And if baking two sheets of cookies at the same time, reverse their positions (top rack to bottom and bottom rack to top) half way through the cooking time so the batch on the bottom rack will not overcook.

For most cookies, it is best to remove them from the cookie sheet while they are still hot, but after they have been allowed to rest for about a minute. Cool the cookies on a rack, if you can.

Always follow directions that say whether pans should be greased or not. In some cases, the butter content and lack of sugar makes greasing unnecessary. In other instances, the opposite is true.

I use a hand-held mixer for making most cookies (page 161) and a rubber spatula (page 168) to clean all the dough out of the mixing bowl.

To store cookies, put them in an airtight jar in layers, separated by sheets of wax paper or cling wrap, and finish off with a sheet of paper on top as well. This is especially important in humid weather and with cookies that are soft or contain beaten egg-white.

When cookies become dried out, don't discard them. Instead, use them to make pie crusts or as topping for ice cream or fresh fruit.

Pecan Lace Cookies

Pecan lace cookies should be a bit brittle, so they can't be underbaked. Test one or two before you bake the whole batch. And if you have any crumbs or crumbled cookies left over, they make a wonderful topping for rich ice cream—something you should remember any time you have cookie crumbs.

When cookie crumbs are soft, lightly toast them before using as a topping.

> 1 cup sifted whole wheat flour
> 1 cup combined chopped pecans and quick-cooking oats (equal portions is good, but more pecans to the mix is okay, too)
> ½ cup light corn syrup
> ½ cup firmly packed dark brown sugar
> ½ cup (1 stick) unsalted butter, softened
> 1 teaspoon vanilla extract

Preheat the oven to 375 degrees. Line 2 cookie sheets with foil (just fold over one end so it stays in place; it is easy to slide off).

On a sheet of wax paper, mix the whole wheat flour, nuts, and oats. Set aside.

In a medium saucepan (nonstick, if you have it), combine the corn syrup, brown sugar, and butter over moderate heat. Bring to a boil, stirring, then remove from heat.

Stir in the vanilla and add the dry ingredients. Stir very thoroughly. The mixture will bubble up and turn opaque.

Drop by tablespoonfuls onto the lined cookie sheet, leaving several inches between for cookies to spread out to make 3- to 4-inch circles.

Bake for 9 minutes, or until set and golden. Remove the cookie sheets from oven and slide the foil onto a cooling rack. Re-line the sheets and continue until you use all the batter.

When completely cooled, peel off foil or store cookies on the foil. When cool, they peel off very easily.

Makes about 30

Above, left to right: *Chocolate Chunk Cookies; Brown Sugar Shortbread; Blowout*

Below, left to right: Coffee-Chocolate-Macadamia Spreads; Cracked Sugar Cookies; Blondies

Blondies

As far as I know, true blondies don't have chocolate in them, but we couldn't resist adding just a little. So these have a chocolate bottom.

It is always important to use good-quality chocolate, such as Lindt or Tobler, in a recipe.

  ½ cup (1 stick) unsalted butter, softened
  1 cup firmly packed light brown sugar
  2 large eggs
  1½ teaspoons vanilla extract
  1 cup sifted cake flour (not self-rising)
  ¼ teaspoon salt
  ⅓ cup coarsely chopped walnuts
  ½ cup coarsely chopped bittersweet chocolate (3-ounce bar)

Preheat the oven to 350 degrees. Butter an 8-inch square baking pan. Set aside.

Cream the butter and brown sugar until fluffy, about 3 minutes. Add the eggs, 1 at a time, beating well after each addition. Stir in the vanilla. Add the flour and salt and beat until well mixed. Fold in the walnuts and then the chocolate pieces. Pour batter into the pan and smooth the top.

Bake in the center of the oven for 30 to 35 minutes, or until a cake tester comes out clean. Cool in the pan before cutting into 2-inch squares.

Makes 16

Blowout

I guess these are called "blowout" because they will blow your taste buds away. They certainly have enough good things in them. A perfect "treat" or gift cookie.

  2 cups sifted all-purpose flour
  1 teaspoon baking soda
  ¼ teaspoon salt
  ½ cup chunky-style peanut butter, at room temperature
  ½ cup (1 stick) unsalted butter, softened
  ½ cup firmly packed light brown sugar
  ¼ cup granulated sugar
  1 large egg
  1 teaspoon vanilla extract
  ¼ cup milk
  ¾ cup semisweet chocolate chips
  ¾ cup honey-roasted peanuts
  ¾ cup coarsely chopped *frozen* miniature peanut butter cups (about 12)

Preheat the oven to 375 degrees.

Combine the flour, baking soda, and salt. Set aside.

Beat the peanut butter and butter together until fluffy. Add the sugars and beat until light and smooth. Then add the egg and beat about 3 minutes. Add the vanilla and mix well. Stir in the flour mixture and beat thoroughly. Sprinkle the milk over the mixture and beat to soften the dough. Fold in the chocolate chips and peanuts, then carefully add the chopped peanut butter cups.

Drop in 2-tablespoon clumps onto an ungreased cookie sheet. Leave enough space between them so they can expand slightly (about 1 inch).

Bake for 10 to 12 minutes, or until just browned. Do not overbake or the cookies will be too dry. Remove with a spatula to a cooling rack. Repeat with remaining batter until used up.

Makes about 30

Brown Sugar Shortbread

Shortbread surely has got to be one of the easiest of all "cookies" to make. And it improves with age. This recipe is a variation on the time-tested classic. I love it with summer drinks.

  1 cup (2 sticks) unsalted butter, softened
  1 cup firmly packed light brown sugar
  1 teaspoon vanilla extract
  2¼ cups sifted all-purpose flour

Preheat the oven to 325 degrees. Butter a 9-inch cake pan and set aside.

Beat the butter, brown sugar, and vanilla together until fluffy, about 3 minutes. Add the flour in 4 batches and combine well after each addition. (You may do this with your hands.) Scrape the dough into the prepared pan and pat into an even layer. Prick the surface with the tines of a fork.

Since shortbread becomes solid when it cools, score the top (do not cut all the way through the dough) before baking so it will be easy to break apart into serving pieces.

Bake in the upper third of the oven for about 30 minutes, or until the top is puffy and lightly browned.

Serves 8

Cracked Sugar Cookies

Cracked sugar cookies get that name from the way their tops look after baking. They have an old-fashioned flavor similar to that of the tea cakes that were so popular years ago.

My Louisiana cousin, Mackie Kyle, gave me this recipe, which she says has been around for a long time.

- 1¼ cups sugar
- 1 cup (2 sticks) unsalted butter, softened
- 3 large egg yolks, lightly beaten
- 1 teaspoon vanilla extract
- 2½ cups sifted all-purpose flour
- 1 teaspoon baking soda
- ½ teaspoon cream of tartar

Preheat the oven to 350 degrees. Lightly grease a cookie sheet.

Cream the sugar and butter until fluffy, about 3 minutes. Beat in the yolks and vanilla. Sift the dry ingredients together, then add to the batter in 4 parts, mixing well after each addition.

Form dough into balls the size of a walnut and place balls on cookie sheet about 2 inches apart. Do not flatten. Bake for approximately 11 minutes. Cool on a wire rack. Repeat with remaining dough until used up.

Makes approximately 4 dozen

Chocolate Chunk Cookies

Chunk is the operative word here, because this recipe calls for coarsely chopped extra-bittersweet chocolate bars. The cookies are similar to the usual chocolate-chip ones, but the larger pieces of chocolate make all the difference.

- 2 cups sifted all-purpose flour
- 1 teaspoon baking soda
- ½ teaspoon salt
- ½ cup (1 stick) plus 2 tablespoons (¼ stick) unsalted butter, softened
- ½ cup firmly packed light brown sugar
- ½ cup firmly packed dark brown sugar
- ¼ cup granulated sugar
- 1 large egg
- 1½ teaspoons vanilla extract
- ¾ cup coarsely chopped walnuts
- 9 ounces extra-bittersweet chocolate (such as 3 Lindt "Traditional" bars), coarsely chopped

Preheat the oven to 375 degrees.

Combine the flour, baking soda, and salt. Set aside.

Cream the butter and sugars until smooth, about 4 minutes. Add the egg and mix well. Add the flour mixture and beat thoroughly. Stir in the vanilla, then fold in the nuts and then the chocolate.

Drop in 2-tablespoon clumps onto an ungreased cookie sheet, leaving several inches between for expansion.

Bake for 10 to 12 minutes, or until the bottoms are lightly browned. Repeat with remaining batter until used up.

Makes approximately 30

Coffee-Chocolate-Macadamia Spreads

I'm really partial to the taste of macadamia nuts. Here they are part of a big, soft, and chewy cookie. Delicious; it's another "treat" or gift cookie.

- 1½ cups sifted whole wheat flour
- ½ teaspoon baking soda
- ¼ teaspoon salt
- ½ cup (1 stick) plus 2 tablespoons (¼ stick) unsalted butter, softened
- 1⅓ cups firmly packed dark brown sugar
- 2 large eggs
- 1 teaspoon vanilla extract
- 1 tablespoon powdered instant espresso
- 3 ounces unsweetened chocolate, melted and cooled to room temperature
- ¾ cup macadamia nuts, halved

Preheat the oven to 350 degrees. Lightly grease 2 cookie sheets. Set aside.

Combine the whole wheat flour, baking soda, and salt. Set aside.

Cream the butter and brown sugar until smooth, about 4 minutes. Add the eggs, 1 at the time, beating well after each addition. Beat in the vanilla and powdered espresso.

Add the flour mixture, one third at the time, beating well after each addition until thoroughly mixed. Blend in the chocolate and fold in the nuts.

Drop in 2-tablespoon clumps onto the prepared sheets, leaving plenty of room for them to spread out. (That's why they are called "spreads.")

Bake for about 12 minutes, or just until soft and lightly crisped around the edges. Remove to a cooling rack. They will harden a bit as they cool.

Makes about 2 dozen

Right: Coconut-Walnut
Jumbles
Below: Fruitcake Cookies
Bottom left: Hazelnut-
Brown Sugar Cookies
Bottom right: Icebox
Cookies
Opposite: Filled Cookies

Coconut-Walnut Jumbles

Coconut jumbles are a long-time favorite and for good reason—they're simple to make and always a hit with the kids. This is a variation on the basic recipe.

- ½ cup (1 stick) plus 2 tablespoons (¼ stick) unsalted butter, softened
- ¾ cup sugar
- 1 large egg
- 1 can (3½ ounces) sweetened grated coconut
- 1 cup sifted all-purpose flour
- ½ teaspoon vanilla extract
- 1 cup coarsely chopped walnuts

Preheat the oven to 425 degrees. Lightly grease a cookie sheet.

Cream the butter and sugar until fluffy, about 3 minutes. Then beat in the egg. Mix coconut and flour in together. This will make a fairly thick batter, but it is easy to mix. Stir in the vanilla and then fold in the nuts. Drop by rounded teaspoonfuls onto the cookie sheet, leaving enough space between cookies for them to expand.

Bake for about 10 minutes, or until cookies turn golden on top. Be careful not to burn bottoms. Remove to a cooling rack. Repeat with remaining batter until used up.

Makes approximately 3 dozen

Filled Cookies

My editor, Carolyn Hart, supplied me with this recipe, which she said was her maternal grandmother's and a family tradition. Try it and you'll see why. Each cookie has a little surprise in the middle. When I made these, it occurred to me that they would be perfect for a picnic.

Incidentally, after you get the hang of making them— and they are quite easy—you can devise your own fillings, using the one here as a guide.

- 3 cups sifted all-purpose flour
- 2 teaspoons baking powder
- ¼ teaspoon salt
- ½ cup (1 stick) unsalted butter, softened
- 1 cup less 2 tablespoons sugar
- 1 large egg
- ½ cup milk
- 1 teaspoon vanilla extract

Filling
- ½ cup chopped raisins
- ¼ cup chopped walnuts
- 3 tablespoons sugar
- ¼ cup water
- ½ teaspoon vanilla extract

Sift the flour, baking powder, and salt together. Set aside.

Beat the butter and sugar together until fluffy, about 3 minutes. Beat the egg lightly and combine with the milk and vanilla. Add to the butter, alternating with the flour mixture and ending with the flour. Beat well after each addition. This will be a fairly sticky dough. Form into a ball, wrap in cling wrap, and put into the freezer for about 1 hour.

Meanwhile, make the filling. Combine all the ingredients except the vanilla and heat until thickened. Off the heat, stir in the vanilla and set aside to cool.

Preheat the oven to 375 degrees.

Divide the dough in half and return the first half to the refrigerator while you work with the other. Place the dough on a well-floured surface and dust with flour. Turn the dough over and make sure there is flour underneath. Roll out thin and cut into 3-inch circles with a floured cutter. As you place a circle on an ungreased cookie sheet, put a generous tablespoon of filling in the center and cover with another circle of dough, pressing the edges together slightly with the tines of a fork. Continue until all the dough and filling are used. Combine the scraps of dough and roll out to make the last cookies.

Bake for about 15 minutes, or until dough begins to brown slightly.

Makes approximately 18 large cookies

Fruitcake Cookies

These cookies, which are wonderful for the holidays, were the idea of my friend and food maven Carole Bannett. The recipe was devised by David Coltin, the moving force behind Society Bakery of Boston, Massachusetts.

This recipe makes about 150 small cookies, but before they are cooked, the dough must be frozen. We have divided the dough in six parts. That way you can take out one part and bake the cookies as you need them.

½ pound dried figs, chopped
¼ pound raisins
¼ pound glacéed cherries, chopped coarsely
1 tablespoon honey
2 tablespoons dry sherry
1 tablespoon lemon juice
Pinch of salt
6 ounces small walnut pieces
1 cup (2 sticks) unsalted butter, softened
½ teaspoon ground cloves
½ cup superfine sugar
⅓ cup firmly packed light brown sugar
1 large egg
2⅔ cups sifted all-purpose flour mixed with ¼ teaspoon salt

Combine the fruits, honey, sherry, lemon juice, salt, and walnuts. Allow to marinate, covered, overnight.

Cream the butter, cloves, and sugars until smooth, about 3 minutes. Add the egg and incorporate. Add the flour and salt mixture in 3 parts, mixing after each addition but being careful not to overmix. Mix in the fruit and nuts, and any liquid. Chill dough briefly, then divide into 6 equal portions and roll into logs with lightly floured hands. Put in freezer for about 1 hour.

Preheat the oven to 350 degrees.

Cut the chilled logs into very thin rounds with a sharp knife and place on an ungreased cookie sheet with about ½ inch between. Bake for 10 to 13 minutes, or until light golden.

Makes about 12½ dozen small cookies

Hazelnut–Brown Sugar Cookies

A lady in Texas sent me this recipe, but I have unfortunately misplaced her name. She said she sometimes makes these delightful cookies with pecans (from her own trees).

1¼ cups sifted all-purpose flour
Dash of salt
¼ teaspoon baking soda
¼ cup (½ stick) unsalted butter, softened
¼ cup (½ stick) margarine, softened
8 ounces light brown sugar
1 large egg
½ teaspoon vanilla extract
1 cup coarsely chopped hazelnuts

Preheat the oven to 350 degrees. Generously grease 2 cookie sheets.

Combine flour with the salt and soda, then sift again. Set aside.

Cream the butter, margarine, and brown sugar until fluffy, about 3 minutes. (If sugar is lumpy, sift before adding.) Add the egg and the vanilla and combine well. Add the dry mixture in 4 parts, mixing well after each addition. Fold in hazelnuts. Drop by teaspoonfuls onto the prepared sheets, leaving room for them to spread.

Bake for 16 to 17 minutes, or until golden. Remove from cookie sheets and cool on a rack. Repeat with remaining batter until used up.

Makes approximately 5 dozen

Icebox Cookies

Icebox cookies take no effort to mix, but must be refrigerated to make handling the dough easier. They may be baked as you need them, however, and supposedly can stay in the refrigerator for up to a week. After that, the flavor begins to deteriorate.

1 cup (2 sticks) unsalted butter, softened
½ cup less 1 tablespoon superfine sugar
1 large egg yolk
½ teaspoon vanilla extract
½ teaspoon almond extract
1¾ cups sifted all-purpose flour
Flavored granulated sugar

Beat the butter and sugar until fluffy, about 3 minutes. Then beat in the egg yolk, vanilla, and almond extract. Stir in the flour in 2 parts, blending well after each addition. Divide the dough in half and roll each half into a 3-inch wide log. Wrap in cling wrap and refrigerate for several hours.

Preheat the oven to 375 degrees.

Using a knife with a very sharp, thin blade, make ⅛-inch dough slices and place them on an ungreased cookie sheet with space between for them to expand. Bake for about 11 minutes, or until they just start to turn color, but not brown. Remove to a rack to cool.

These cookies are already rather sweet, but you could sprinkle them with flavored granulated sugar after they have cooled slightly, if you like. Repeat with remaining dough until used up.

Makes approximately 3 dozen

Top: Meringue Nut
Cookies
Above: Molasses Cookies
Right: Milk Chocolate
Macaroons

<u>Left</u>: Oatmeal-Raisin
Cookies
<u>Below</u>: Lemon Squares

Lemon Squares

Here's another recipe from my editor, Carolyn Hart, this one from her Auntie Pearl, to be exact. And they are scrumptious.

At this writing, Auntie Pearl is eighty-four and still going strong. Long may she wave.

- 1 cup (2 sticks) unsalted butter, softened
- 2 cups plus 1 tablespoon sifted all-purpose flour
- ½ cup sifted confectioners' sugar
- 4 large eggs, at room temperature
- 2 cups granulated sugar
- Grated rind of 1 large lemon
- 6 tablespoons lemon juice
- ½ teaspoon baking powder
- 1½ cups chopped walnuts

Preheat the oven to 325 degrees. Grease a 9 x 13-inch baking pan. Set aside.

Beat together the butter, 2 cups of flour, and the confectioners' sugar until fluffy. Scrape mixture into the prepared pan and smooth into a thin layer covering the bottom. Bake for 15 minutes.

Meanwhile, beat the eggs and sugar until light. Add lemon rind and juice, and mix. Sprinkle the tablespoon of flour and the ½ teaspoon of baking powder over all, then pour in the nuts. Combine well.

Pour lemon mixture into crust and return to oven to bake for another 35 minutes, or until filling is set.

Let cool slightly, then cut into squares. Loosen crust around the edges before removing squares from the pan.

Makes approximately 2 dozen

Meringue Nut Cookies

This is a recipe from my fellow food enthusiast Jean Thackery. It makes a cookie that literally melts in your mouth. Try them with homemade strawberry ice cream.

Incidentally, this is a good way to use some of those egg whites we occasionally wind up with and feel too guilty to throw out.

- 3 large egg whites, at room temperature
- ⅛ teaspoon salt
- ½ teaspoon cream of tartar
- ¾ cup sugar
- 2 cups coarsely chopped nuts—walnuts, pecans, hazelnuts, or a combination

Preheat the oven to 200 degrees. Lightly butter, then barely flour a sheet of parchment (or wax) paper. Place paper on a cookie sheet and set aside.

Beat the egg whites until foamy. Add the salt and cream of tartar and continue beating until stiff. Stir in sugar gradually and, finally, fold in nuts carefully.

Drop batter onto the lined cookie sheet. The cookies do not rise or spread much, so they can be placed fairly close together, but not touching.

Bake for 1 to 1¼ hours, or until just very slightly browned. Allow to cool, then carefully peel off the paper. Repeat for remaining batter until used up.

Makes approximately 3 dozen

Milk Chocolate Macaroons

Everyone knows macaroons, but when made with milk chocolate they become something else altogether. If milk chocolate is not your taste, change it to bittersweet. They are great with a glass of cold milk.

- 3 large egg whites, at room temperature
- Pinch of salt
- ⅔ cup superfine sugar
- 1 teaspoon vanilla extract
- 6 ounces milk chocolate, melted and cooled to room temperature
- 2 cans (3½ ounces each) sweetened grated coconut (about 2⅓ cups)

Preheat the oven to 325 degrees. Line 2 cookie sheets with foil, then lightly grease the foil and set aside.

Whisk the egg whites with the salt until they form soft peaks. Gradually add the sugar a little at the time, whisking at high speed all the while, until very stiff but not dry. Quickly fold in the vanilla and chocolate, then fold in the coconut.

Drop in 1½-inch clumps on the prepared sheets, leaving an inch or so between for spreading.

Bake for 20 to 22 minutes, or until set, but with peaks only lightly browned. Remove from foil and let cool on a rack. Store in an airtight jar.

Makes about 30

Molasses Cookies

Mrs. Curtis McCaskill sent this recipe to me from Mississippi, where they know all about molasses.

The black pepper gives these cookies an interesting bite. But you wouldn't know what you were tasting unless you were told.

¾ cup sugar, plus additional for coating
¾ cup (1½ sticks) unsalted butter, softened
1 large egg
¼ cup unsulphured molasses
2 cups sifted all-purpose flour
2 teaspoons baking soda
½ teaspoon salt
1 tablespoon ground allspice
1 teaspoon ground cinnamon
1 teaspoon black pepper

Preheat the oven to 350 degrees.

Cream the sugar and butter until fluffy, about 3 minutes. Beat in the egg and then add the molasses. Combine the flour with the other dry ingredients and sift again. Add to dough and mix well.

Form dough into 1-inch balls and roll in additional sugar. Place 2 inches apart on an ungreased cookie sheet.

Bake for 12 to 15 minutes, or until set. Repeat with remaining dough until used up.

Makes approximately 4 dozen

Oatmeal-Raisin Cookies

Pamela Krausmann, who has got to be one of the best and most knowledgeable food people around, created this recipe, which makes the best oatmeal raisin cookies I've had.

1½ cups sifted all-purpose flour
1 teaspoon baking soda
1 teaspoon ground cinnamon
1 cup (2 sticks) unsalted butter, softened
½ cup firmly packed dark brown sugar
1 cup granulated sugar
1 large egg, well beaten
1 teaspoon vanilla extract
1½ cups old-fashioned rolled oats
1 cup raisins

Sift together the flour, baking soda, and cinnamon. Set aside.

Cream the butter and sugars until fluffy, about 3 minutes. Mix the beaten egg in thoroughly, then stir in the vanilla. Add the dry mixture. Mix in the oatmeal and then the raisins. Give it a final mixing. Refrigerate, covered, for 1 hour.

Preheat the oven to 350 degrees. Grease a cookie sheet.

Place walnut-size pieces of dough on the prepared sheet, allowing space for cookies to spread.

Bake for 10 minutes, or until set. Repeat for remaining dough until used up.

Makes approximately 5 dozen

Above: Snickerdoodles
Left: Rocks
Below: Spice Sablés
Bottom: Praline Cookies
Right: Outrageous Brownies

Outrageous Brownies

If ever a cookie was aptly named, this one is. They are certainly outrageous—outrageously good. I know there are a million versions of brownies, but this one by Ina Garten certainly ranks with the very best. Perfect with homemade vanilla ice cream or cold milk or bourbon whipped cream (page 150) or at midnight.

Thanks, Ina; you are going to make a lot of people happy.

  1 pound (4 sticks) unsalted butter
  1 pound plus 3 cups semisweet chocolate chips
  6 ounces unsweetened chocolate
  6 large eggs
  2 tablespoons plus 1½ teaspoons powdered instant espresso
  2 tablespoons vanilla extract
2¼ cups sugar
  1 cup sifted all-purpose flour
  1 tablespoon baking powder
  1 teaspoon salt
  3 cups chopped walnut pieces

Preheat the oven to 350 degrees. Grease and flour a 12 x 18-inch jelly-roll pan. Set aside.

Melt together the butter, pound of chocolate chips, and unsweetened chocolate until smooth in the top of a double broiler. Cool to room temperature

Combine, but do not whisk, the eggs, powdered espresso, vanilla, and sugar. Stir in the cooled chocolate mixture. Set aside.

Sift together the flour, baking powder, and salt. Mix into the batter. Finally, fold in the remaining chocolate chips and the walnuts. Pour into the greased pan.

Bake about 30 minutes, or until a tester just comes out clean. Do not overbake. Cool thoroughly and cut into squares.

Note: Half way through baking, open the oven, lift the pan, and smack it on the rack. Turn the pan around and smack the other side: This stops the rising process and gives the brownies their sinfully dense texture.

Makes 20

Rocks

This recipe came from a Texan woman named Susie Jastro, and was part of a booklet put together by her family to celebrate the eighty-first birthday of their cook, Anna Glover. By then, Anna had worked for the family for almost forty years. She is still spry at eighty-six, though no longer baking these crowd-pleasing cookies very often.

I've cut the original recipe in half; otherwise these are just as she made them.

2¾ cups sifted all-purpose flour
  1 teaspoon baking soda
  ½ teaspoon ground cinnamon
  ½ teaspoon ground nutmeg
  ½ teaspoon grated orange rind
  ½ cup (1 stick) unsalted butter, softened
1½ cups firmly packed dark brown sugar
  2 tablespoons milk
  2 large eggs, lightly beaten
  1 cup raisins
  1 cup currants
  4 ounces pitted dates, coarsely chopped
  ¾ cup coarsely chopped walnuts

Preheat the oven to 300 degrees.

Set aside ¼ cup of the flour. Sift the balance with the baking soda, cinnamon, and nutmeg. Sprinkle the grated orange rind over the top and set aside.

Cream the butter and sugar until smooth, about 2 minutes. Add the milk and eggs, mixing well. Stir in the flour mixture in 4 parts, mixing thoroughly after each addition. Set aside.

Mix the raisins, currants, dates, and nuts and toss well with the reserved flour. Fold these (along with any extra flour) into the batter. Drop in rounded tablespoonfuls onto ungreased cookie sheets.

Bake for 23 to 25 minutes, or until very slightly browned. Remove with a spatula to a cooling rack.

Makes about 50

Praline Cookies

A friend of my Aunt Freddie's in Natchez, Mississippi, gave me this recipe. It makes delicious crunchy treats and is simple to do.

Incidentally, I make these and all other cookies (such as the whole wheat benne wafers on page 142) on parchment, as I was told to do by a professional cookie chef. You can't beat parchment for making it easy to remove the cookies.

1 cup firmly packed light brown sugar, sifted
1 large egg white, stiffly beaten
2 cups coarsely chopped pecans
1 teaspoon vanilla extract

Preheat the oven to 275 degrees. Grease (or spray with vegetable cooking spray) 2 sheets of parchment paper and place them on cookie sheets.

Sift the brown sugar, then add to the beaten egg white and mix well. Stir in the nuts and vanilla. Drop by teaspoonfuls onto the lined cookie sheets and bake for approximately 30 minutes, or until set and golden. Carefully remove cookies from parchment, using a spatula while they are still hot. Cool on rack. (If you allow them to cool on the sheet, they will break apart as you try to remove them.)

Makes approximately 3 dozen

Spice Sablés

These meltingly good rolled cookies are the brainchild of talented pastry chef André Fecteau, who turns the tempting and palate-teasing delicacies at the Barefoot Contessa in the Hamptons.

2 cups sifted all-purpose flour
1½ teaspoons ground cinnamon
½ teaspoon grated nutmeg
½ teaspoon ground allspice
¾ (1½ sticks) unsalted butter, softened
½ teaspoon salt
½ cup firmly packed light brown sugar
2 tablespoons Grand Marnier
½ cup finely ground blanched almonds

Sift together the flour, cinnamon, nutmeg, and allspice. Set aside.

Cream the butter, salt, and brown sugar until smooth. Stir in the Grand Marnier and then the almonds. Beat in the dry mixture and pat into a ball. Wrap in cling wrap and refrigerate for 1 hour.

Preheat the oven to 325 degrees. Grease and flour several cookie sheets. Roll out and pat the dough (it will not stretch like pie or biscuit dough, but is more grainy) on a floured surface until ¼ inch thick. Cut into cookies with a 3-inch floured cookie cutter in the shape of your choice. Place on prepared cookie sheet.

Bake for 15 to 20 minutes, or until lightly browned. Remove to a cooling rack.

Makes about 2 dozen

Snickerdoodles

A true American classic. And heaven only knows how these cookies really got their name, although I'm sure many people will swear they know.

I've found that at least a dozen snickerdoodles disappear as soon as they come out of the oven. And the ones that are left don't fare much better. That tells you something.

I think most of us secretly think that anything we eat standing up in the kitchen doesn't count.

2¾ cups sifted all-purpose flour
2 teaspoons cream of tartar
1 teaspoon baking soda
¼ teaspoon salt
1 cup (2 sticks) unsalted butter, softened
1½ cups sugar plus ¼ cup sugar mixed with 1 tablespoon ground cinnamon
2 large eggs

Combine the flour, cream of tartar, baking soda, and salt and sift again. Set aside.

Cream the butter and sugar until fluffy, about 3 minutes. Add the eggs, 1 at a time, beating well after each addition. Add the flour mixture in 4 parts and beat thoroughly after adding each part.

Wrap dough in plastic and refrigerate for at least 1 hour.

Preheat the oven to 400 degrees.

Roll dough into balls about the size of a walnut, then roll each in the sugar-cinnamon mixture. Place about 2 inches apart on an ungreased cookie sheet.

Bake for 8 to 10 minutes, or until just lightly browned, but still soft. Repeat until remaining dough is used up.

Makes about 3 dozen

<u>Top to bottom:</u>
Texas Peanut-Bran Cookies;
Thumbprint Cookies;
Vermont Ginger
and Spice Cookies

140

Top: Vanilla Crescents
Bottom: Whole Wheat Benne Wafers

Texas Peanut-Bran Cookies

This is a Texas cookie because it came from a friend of my aunt in Texas. You can use a state of your choice when referring to its origin.

    1½   cups sifted all-purpose flour
    1   teaspoon baking powder
    ¾   teaspoon baking soda
    ½   teaspoon salt
    ½   cup (1 stick) unsalted butter, softened
    1¼   cups firmly packed dark brown sugar
    1   large egg
    1   teaspoon vanilla extract
    ¼   cup milk
    1½   cups bran flakes cereal
    1   cup coarsely chopped salted peanuts

Preheat the oven to 375 degrees. Grease 2 cookie sheets. Set aside.

Sift together the flour, baking powder, baking soda, and salt. Set aside.

Cream the butter and brown sugar until fluffy, about 3 minutes. Add the egg and vanilla, beating well. Alternate adding the dry mixture and milk in several parts, mixing well after each addition. Stir in the bran and the nuts. Drop by tablespoonfuls onto the prepared cookie sheets, leaving enough room for them to spread out. Bake about 15 minutes.

Makes approximately 4 dozen

Thumbprint Cookies

The little rush of sweet jelly on top of these cookies hits the spot. A good dessert cookie.

Of course, you can use any kind of jam you particularly like.

    ½   cup (1 stick) unsalted butter, softened
    ⅓   cup sugar
    2   large eggs, separated, at room temperature
    1   teaspoon vanilla extract
    ½   teaspoon salt
    1½   cups sifted all-purpose flour
    1   cup finely chopped walnuts or pecans
         About 1 cup raspberry or blackberry jelly or
         jam

Preheat the oven to 350 degrees. Grease 2 cookie sheets. Set aside.

Cream the butter and sugar until fluffy, about 3 minutes. Add the egg yolks 1 at a time, mixing well after each addition. Stir in the vanilla and salt.

Gradually add the flour and mix well.

To assemble, lightly whip the egg whites with a fork. Place nuts in another bowl. Shape dough into ¾- to 1-inch balls, and dip each ball in egg white and then roll in nuts. Place 1 inch apart on the prepared cookie sheets. Use your thumb to make a deep depression in the middle of each. (Thumbprint cookies, get it?)

Bake for 15 to 17 minutes, or until lightly browned and firm. Let cool on a wire rack. Fill each cookie with ½ teaspoon of jam. Store cookies in an airtight container.

Makes about 3 dozen

Whole Wheat Benne Wafers

For those of you who don't know, benne seeds are sesame seeds. The African name for these seeds is used in the South.

The whole wheat flour used here instead of traditional white flour is a nutritional update.

    ⅔   cup sifted whole wheat flour
         Pinch of salt
    ¼   teaspoon baking powder
    ½   cup (1 stick) unsalted butter, softened
    1   cup firmly packed light brown sugar
    1   large egg
    1   teaspoon vanilla extract
    1¼   cups sesame (benne) seeds, toasted*

Preheat the oven to 350 degrees. Lightly grease several sheets of cooking parchment. Put them on cookie sheets and set aside.

Combine the whole wheat flour, salt, and baking powder and set aside.

Cream the butter and brown sugar until fluffy, about 3 minutes. Add the egg and vanilla and combine well. Add the dry mixture, beating just enough to combine. Then stir in the sesame seeds.

Drop by small teaspoonfuls onto the lined sheets, leaving 2 inches in between. These spread and become very thin. If you bake 2 cookie sheets at once, reverse them halfway through the cooking time.

Bake for 6 to 8 minutes, or until lightly browned. Allow cookies to cool on the sheet for about 30 seconds, then gently remove them to a cooling rack. To preserve their crispness, store in an airtight jar.

Makes approximately 6 dozen

* To toast sesame seeds, place them in a cold skillet over moderate heat. Stir and shake until golden. Do not overcook, as they will give up too much of their oil and become bitter.

Vanilla Crescents

I suspect everyone's had a version of this cookie, as it crops up in some form or another in all cuisines.

This particular recipe was given by Grandmother Haidin to Mardee Regan's mother when she married. Mardee has simplified it even more by chopping the vanilla bean and nuts in the processor at the same time, then adding the rest of the ingredients for a quick whirl. A breeze to make.

   ¼ cup sugar plus 2 cups for coating
   1 vanilla bean, crushed and broken into chunks
   ½ cup shelled walnuts
   1 cup (2 sticks) unsalted butter, softened
  2⅓ cups sifted all-purpose flour

Preheat the oven to 350 degrees.

Place ¼ cup of the sugar and the vanilla bean in the bowl of a food processor fitted with a metal blade. Pulse off and on a few times to chop the bean, then add the walnuts. Process until finely chopped. Add the butter and flour and process, scraping down sides of the bowl, until dough is pliable. Remove and gather into a ball.

Pinch off walnut-size pieces of dough and shape into balls. Then shape balls into small crescents about the size of your thumb. Place crescents ½ inch apart on an ungreased cookie sheet (these do not expand).

Bake for 10 minutes, then reduce the oven temperature to 300 degrees and bake for an additional 10 to 15 minutes, or until cookies are tan and dry.

Roll the hot cookies in sugar and let cool on wire racks.

Makes about 3 dozen

Vermont Ginger and Spice Cookies

These are semisoft cookies. The recipe comes from someone who wrote to me from Vermont years ago. Sad to say, I no longer know who it was.

I make them medium-size, but these cookies could be made larger. Just give them room to spread.

   4 cups sifted all-purpose flour
   ¾ teaspoon baking soda
   ¾ teaspoon ground ginger
  1½ teaspoons ground cinnamon
  1½ teaspoons ground cloves
   ½ teaspoon salt
   1 cup (2 sticks) unsalted butter, softened
  1¼ cups sugar, plus additional for coating
   ½ cup unsulphured molasses
   2 medium eggs
   1 teaspoon vanilla extract

Preheat the oven to 350 degrees.

Sift together the flour, baking soda, ginger, cinnamon, cloves, and salt. Set aside.

Cream the butter with the sugar until fluffy, about 3 minutes. Stir in the molasses and mix in the eggs, 1 at a time, stirring thoroughly after each addition. Stir in vanilla.

Add the dry mixture in 3 parts, mixing thoroughly after each addition.

Pour out the remaining sugar on a piece of wax paper. Using 2 tablespoons, drop walnut-size lumps of dough onto the sugar and roll around to coat. Place on an ungreased cookie sheet 2 inches apart. Bake for 14 minutes or until light golden. Remove to a cooling rack. Continue to make remaining cookies until dough is used up.

Makes approximately 5 dozen

Candies

I have not had much of a career as a candy
maker, so this section is put together with recipes collected from the few people I know who
do enjoy making it. Several years ago, I wanted to
try my hand at pecan brittle. I must say that I liked
doing that, so maybe there is hope for me yet.

Or course, like everyone else, when I was a kid
we tried making fudge, which usually turned out
more like a brick than a confection, but it was sweet
and that was all that counted. And I remember my
paternal grandmother, who was a very good cook
otherwise, used to attempt making divinity—usually
around Christmas and mostly with the same sticky
results each time. Someone had told her along the
way that lemon juice helped stabilize it, so she
always gave hers a shot of that; the only kind I knew
was (inadvertently) lemon divinity, which is not
recommended unless you are a child, in which case
anything goes. As a matter of fact, it wasn't until I
had divinity made by Mrs. Sloan Smith (receipe follows) that I found out how good this white candy
can be.

Maybe the reason candy didn't interest me earlier
is that the results were always so iffy. But when the
candy thermometer came into general use and
stopped being an exotic kitchen accessory, the
guesswork more or less left candy making. Before, I
suppose you just had to make candy often enough to
know what degree of softness a soft ball in water had
to have or you would burn the kitchen to the
ground and permanently ruin a saucepan while making toffee.

Being from Louisiana, I have had my share of pra-
lines, both good and not so good. However, the recipe in this chapter is from my Aunt Freddie and is a
good one.

Speaking of Aunt Freddie, the other kind of
candy I remember her trying (and *trying* is the operative word here) was pull taffy. I think she just liked
the idea of a taffy pull, because nobody seemed to
care too much for its taste—even the children. But
attempt it she did, for her daughter and her friends.
My memory of these episodes is of what a mess it all
was. Even on those occasions when the taffy was
more or less the right consistency it was always too
hot to handle, buttered hands not withstanding.
Maybe just doing it was the point, after all. It kept a
lot of 7- and 8-year-old girls occupied. You won't
find a recipe for pull taffy here.

Anyway, get out your candy thermometer and
give some of these recipes a try. Personally, I
wouldn't try making candy without one.

Black Walnut Divinity

Mrs. Sloan Smith (none other than columnist Liz Smith's mother) has been making this divinity at Christmas ever since anybody can remember—almost literally, since Mrs. Smith is now in her nineties and still going strong.

- 2½ cups sugar
- ½ cup water
- ½ cup light corn syrup
- 2 large egg whites, at room temperature
  Pinch of salt
- 1 cup black (or English) walnuts or pecans, coarsely chopped
- 1 teaspoon vanilla extract

Generously grease a 12-inch plate.

Combine sugar, water, and corn syrup in a small pan and bring to a boil. Continue boiling until syrup makes a firm ball, 249 degrees on a candy thermometer. While syrup is cooking, beat the egg whites with the salt until they form soft peaks.

When the syrup is the right temperature, pour about half of it into the whites, beating all the while. Return the balance of the syrup to the heat and cook until it reaches the hard-ball stage, 260 degrees. Pour, in a steady stream, into the egg-white mixture, beating all the while. Continue to beat for a few minutes, then fold in the nuts and vanilla. Pour into prepared plate and allow to cool. Cut into squares while lukewarm.

When completely cool, wrap individual pieces in cling wrap, since divinity will harden if left exposed to the air.

Makes approximately 18 pieces

Chocolate Fudge

This is Liz Smith's (of the famous candy-making Smiths) own fudge. Years ago we used to make it in the country to finish off the Saturday evening festivities. Young and foolish, you know.

- 2 cups sugar
- 2 heaping tablespoons unsweetened cocoa powder
- 1 cup milk
  Dash of salt
- ¼ cup (½ stick) unsalted butter, cut into bits
- 2 teaspoons vanilla extract

Generously grease a 12-inch plate.

Mix sugar, cocoa, milk, and salt in a small saucepan and bring to a boil over medium heat, stirring occasionally. Boil until it reaches the soft-ball stage, 240 degrees on a candy thermometer.

Stir in the butter and vanilla and continue to beat until candy begins to set. Quickly turn into prepared plate. When set, cut into squares.

Makes approximately 18 pieces

Chocolate-Nut Toffee

Chocolate-nut toffee is the invention of John Prescott's mother. Together they own a confection company called Katherine's Own. This particular candy was made exclusively for me to sell at Saks Fifth Avenue—and what a hit it was.

Actually, the doing of this candy is rather tedious, but now when you buy toffee, you will know how much loving care goes into its making.

- 1 pound (4 sticks) lightly salted butter
- 2 cups sugar
- 1 cup slivered almonds
- 4 ounces semisweet chocolate
- 4 ounces bittersweet chocolate
- 1 cup chopped pecans

Combine the butter and sugar in a large saucepan and bring to a boil over medium heat. Stirring with an over-and-under motion (like folding egg whites into a batter), cook until sugar is dissolved. Add almonds and continue to cook, stirring with the same motion all the while, until mixture reaches the hard-crack stage, 300 degrees on the candy thermometer; it will be smoking and dark brown. This can take from 45 minutes to 1 hour.

Pour out onto a marble slab or into a jelly-roll pan and allow to harden for about 6 hours.

Melt the chocolates together and spread evenly over the top of the toffee. Sprinkle with the chopped pecans, and allow to rest for several hours. Break into pieces, and store in an airtight container.

Makes approximately 3 pounds

Nut Brittle

I'll go out on a limb and say that this is my favorite simple candy. If you have never made it, try it.

        2   cups pecan or walnut pieces or
            whole peanuts
        1   cup sugar
        1   cup light corn syrup
        1   tablespoon baking soda

Butter a cookie sheet and set aside (or coat with nonstick spray). Combine nuts, sugar, and corn syrup in a medium saucepan set over medium heat. Bring to a boil, stirring constantly, then allow to boil, without stirring, until the mixture reaches the hard-crack stage, 295 degrees on a candy thermometer.

Remove saucepan from the heat and stir in the baking soda. This will foam up; mix quickly and then pour onto prepared cookie sheet.

When cool enough to handle, stretch the brittle to get it as thin as possible. Allow to cool completely and break into pieces. Store in an airtight container.

Makes about 1¼ pounds

Pralines

This is my Aunt Freddie's recipe. There are many others to choose from, but all are very similar.

        2   cups granulated sugar
        1   cup firmly packed dark brown sugar
        ½   cup (1 stick) unsalted butter
        1   cup milk
        2   tablespoons light corn syrup
        4   cups pecan halves and pieces

In a large saucepan, combine the sugars, butter, milk, and corn syrup. Bring to a boil over medium heat, and continue, stirring occasionally, until mixture reaches soft-ball stage, 240 degrees on a candy thermometer; this will take about 20 minutes. After the mixture has been boiling for about 10 minutes, stir in the pecans and continue to cook to required temperature.

Drop by tablespoonfuls onto wax paper and let cool.

Makes about 18

Mamie Eisenhower Fudge

I don't know if this really was Mamie's recipe, but I've always heard it referred to that way. (Well, that's better than being remembered for funny little bangs hanging down from under your hat.)

        4½ cups sugar
            Pinch of salt
        2   tablespoons (¼ stick) unsalted butter
        1   can (12 ounces) evaporated milk
        2   cups semisweet chocolate chips
        2   cups milk chocolate chips
        1   jar (7½ ounces) marshmallow cream
        2   cups coarsely chopped walnuts

Combine the sugar, salt, butter, and milk in a large saucepan and bring to a boil over medium heat. Simmer to soft-ball stage, or until a candy thermometer reaches 240 degrees.

Meanwhile, combine the chocolate chips and marshmallow cream in a large bowl. Butter a 9 x 13-inch pan.

When the sugar mixture is ready, add the chocolate mixture and mix until chocolates are melted and the mixture is smooth. Stir in walnuts quickly, and pour into prepared pan. Allow to cool and cut into squares.

Makes a whopping 5 pounds

Peanut Butter Fudge

Who doesn't remember the taste of this old standby? Often the peanut butter was combined with chocolate, but here it stands alone. A winner both ways.

        2   cups sugar
        ¾   cup milk
        ½   teaspoon salt
        1   teaspoon vanilla extract
        2   tablespoons (¼ stick) unsalted butter
        6   tablespoons chunky-style peanut butter

Generously butter a 12-inch plate.

Combine the sugar, milk, and salt in a small saucepan. Over medium heat, boil slowly to the soft-ball stage, 240 degrees on the candy thermometer. Off the heat, stir in the vanilla, butter, and peanut butter. Mix well and pour onto a buttered plate. Let cool, then cut into squares.

Makes about 2 dozen pieces

Sauces and Toppings

Bourbon Whipped Cream

Butterscotch Sauce

Brandy Sauce

Chocolate Sauce

Chocolate Whipped Cream

Fruit Sauce

Irish Coffee Sauce

Praline Sauce

Rum-Fig Sauce

Vanilla Custard Sauce

S auces and toppings have been sorely
neglected, in my opinion. Easy to make,
they have many more uses than just dressing
up ice cream. So give them a little attention.

For instance, if you have leftover cake or custard,
you can completely transform it with the addition of
a sauce or a flavored whipped cream. Think what
English trifle is made from: just miscellaneous ingredients, all of which seem to be handy leftovers. And
think how *good* it is once it is all put together.

In season, of course, berries and other wonderful
ripe fruits need only puréeing with a little sweetener
and some lemon juice to become a perfect dessert
topping. And with the advent of the food processor
this task involves nothing more than peeling the
fruit and flicking the switch.

Such sauces are also a marvelous opportunity to
utilize frozen fruits of all kinds. Since freezing
destroys the texture of fruits, sauces are an ideal way
to still enjoy their flavor. It is fortunate that fruit
sauces are so simple to prepare, since they are really
at their best when fresh. Don't try making them too
far in advance, or they will deteriorate. Some
uncooked fruit sauces even begin to ferment and
turn sour after only half a day or so, while the old
standbys like chocolate, butterscotch, praline, and
simple cooked syrups will keep refrigerated for weeks
in an airtight container. Also, pressing some cling
wrap directly onto the surface of thicker sauces helps
prevent a film from forming on top.

Although they are not mentioned in the recipes,
crumbs make good toppings or additions to toppings. If you have stale cookies, crumble or grind
them and combine them with ground nuts, then
sprinkle the mixture over creamy desserts. Or use
them to give texture to a smooth topping like chocolate sauce. For this, don't combine the two, but
put the smooth topping on first and finish it off with
the crunchy one.

And by using several compatible toppings on the
same dessert you can create something entirely new
—for instance, chocolate sauce topped with fresh
strawberry purée and sprinkled with nut-cookie
crumbs. Vanilla ice cream will never be the same.

Finally, if you like spirits and liqueurs, they can
give desserts added zing, as I suggested doing when
serving the pear ice on page 11, for instance. In that
case, make a hollow in the top of the scoop of ice,
then fill it with pear brandy. Or sprinkle cakes and
custards with spirits before the other sauces go on.

Vanilla-Bean Custard Ice Cream with Rum-Fig Sauce

Bourbon Whipped Cream

This is nothing more than whipped cream to which bourbon is added. The proportions are up to you, but I like to add 1 teaspoon of sugar to 1 cup of cream as it is being whipped, and then stir in about 2 tablespoons of bourbon when the whipping is finished.

Bourbon whipped cream is marvelous on most cobblers and fruit desserts, as well as on simple cakes.

Of course, whipped cream may be flavored with other liquors, such as rum, as well as liqueurs and fruit brandies, such as poire or calvados.

Butterscotch Sauce

This is perfect over ice cream, sprinkled with nuts.

- 1 cup firmly packed light brown sugar
- ¼ cup half-and-half
- 2 tablespoons light corn syrup
- 2 tablespoons (¼ stick) unsalted butter
- ½ teaspoon vanilla extract

Combine the brown sugar, half-and-half, corn syrup, and butter in a small saucepan over low heat. Bring to a boil slowly, stirring until thickened, about 4 to 5 minutes. Remove from heat and stir in the vanilla. Allow to cool before refrigerating.

Makes about 1½ cups

Brandy Sauce

I like this sauce on fresh fruit, as well as on ice cream or custard.

- 2 large egg yolks, at room temperature
- ¼ cup sugar
- 3 tablespoons brandy (or liqueur)
- 1 cup heavy cream, whipped

Beat together the egg yolks and sugar until light in color and sugar has dissolved. Add the brandy and mix thoroughly. Fold mixture into the whipped cream. Chill for at least 3 hours before serving.

Makes 2 cups

Chocolate Sauce

I don't have to explain chocolate sauce. We all grew up on it.

- 6 ounces semisweet chocolate, or 4 ounces semisweet and 2 ounces unsweetened
- ½ cup light corn syrup
- ¼ cup half-and-half or cream
- 1 tablespoon unsalted butter
- ½ teaspoon vanilla extract

Coarsely chop the chocolate, then melt it over hot water in the top of a double boiler along with the syrup. Mix well, and add half-and-half. Blend well, and stir in the butter. Remove pan from heat and add vanilla and mix.

Serve warm or allow to cool and refrigerate.

Makes about 1½ cups

Rum-Fig Sauce

Rum-fig sauce is a particular favorite of mine. It can turn the most unassuming little custard into a treat.

- 1 cup coarsely chopped dried (or fresh) figs
- ½ cup dark rum
- 1 tablespoon grated lemon rind
- 1½ cups sugar
- 6 tablespoons water
- ½ cup heavy cream

Place the figs in a small bowl, add rum, and sprinkle with the lemon rind. Mix well, then set aside and allow to marinate for at least 1 hour.

Combine the sugar and water in a small, heavy-bottomed saucepan. Bring to a boil over high heat, then turn heat down to medium. Allow to boil slowly until syrup starts to turn golden, about 10 to 15 minutes.

Meanwhile, put a kettle of water on to heat. Drain off any rum that has not been absorbed by the figs and mix with the cream. When syrup starts to caramelize, quickly add the rum-cream mixture off the heat and stir to dissolve the caramel. Set the saucepan in a larger bowl and surround with medium-hot water as you stir if the caramel is not dissolving fast enough. Add the figs and mix thoroughly. Serve warm or at room temperature.

Makes about 3 generous cups

Irish Coffee Sauce

Irish coffee sauce is marvelous on chocolate angel food cake (see page 30) or any chocolate dessert. It's also good with plain custards.

- 1 cup sugar
- 7 tablespoons water
- 1 cup freshly made strong coffee
- 2 tablespoons Irish whiskey or bourbon

Put the sugar and water in a medium to large saucepan and bring to a boil over medium heat. Simmer, stirring until the mixture begins to turn a caramel color, about 10 minutes. Toward the end of the cooking, the mixture will become very foamy as it starts to darken. Stir constantly at this point and, just as it becomes medium caramel color, turn off the heat but continue to stir—it will become darker off the heat. Add the coffee, being careful since the mixture tends to spatter when the coffee first makes contact (the reason for the large pan). Mix well and let cool. Stir in the whiskey and refrigerate.

Makes about 2¼ cups

Vanilla Custard Sauce

Serve this on simple sliced cake or warm fruit.

- 2 cups half-and-half
- 1 vanilla bean
- 3 large eggs
- ¼ cup sugar
- ¼ teaspoon salt

Place the half-and-half and the vanilla bean in the top of a double boiler. Heat to the boiling point, then take from the heat and remove the vanilla bean. Slit the bean open and scrape the seeds out into the half-and-half. (Dry off the bean and use it to flavor granulated sugar.)

Beat the eggs with a fork, then add the sugar and salt. Mix well, and add a few tablespoons of hot half-and-half to warm the eggs. Put half-and-half back over barely simmering water and stir in the warmed egg mixture. Continue to cook, stirring constantly, until the custard coats spoon.

Remove pan from the heat and press a sheet of wax paper or cling wrap onto the surface of the custard to keep a film from forming. Allow to cool completely before refrigerating.

Makes about 2½ cups

Chocolate Whipped Cream

- 1 ounce unsweetened chocolate, coarsely chopped
- ¼ cup sugar
- 1 cup heavy cream

Place the chocolate, sugar, and 2 tablespoons of the cream in the top of a double boiler. Melt over simmering water, then cool by beating. Set aside.

Whip the balance of the cream and add to the cooled chocolate mixture. Combine gently.

Makes 1½ cups

Praline Sauce

- 2 cups cane syrup
- ⅓ cup boiling water
- ⅓ cup firmly packed dark brown sugar
- 1 cup coarsely chopped pecans
- ½ teaspoon vanilla extract

Combine all ingredients except vanilla in a saucepan. Bring to a boil over medium heat, stirring, and allow to boil for about 30 seconds. Remove from heat, and stir in vanilla. Cool, then refrigerate.

Makes about 3 generous cups

Fruit Sauce

A sauce that's perfect for custards and ice cream can be made from almost any fruit or combination of fruits. Something else to recommend this sauce is that it can be prepared from frozen fruit, making it cheaper than using fresh produce. This is especially true of raspberries or blackberries.

For a berry sauce, add ¼ to ½ cup of sugar to a pint of fresh or frozen berries and simmer until mixture starts to thicken, about 5 minutes. Allow to cool and refrigerate.

For a fruit sauce such as from peaches, peel and pit the fruit, then add sugar to taste and a squeeze of lemon juice. Simmer for 5 or more minutes, then purée in a food processor and allow to cool before refrigerating.

You may also add a bit of grated lemon rind to the finished purée as well as a dash of liqueur.

Kids'
Desserts

Previous page: Popcorn Balls

My method of selecting the desserts, or treats, to include in this chapter was very unscientific, so it is possible that your favorite childhood treat has been overlooked. I asked my friends, and anyone else I happened to remember to question, to name their favorite childhood desserts. Not grown-up things or complicated cakes and pies or ice cream, but those sweets made specifically with children in mind.

There wasn't much of this sort of thing in my family, except for popcorn balls, which I still love. Maybe that's because we always had really good regular desserts. In any case, I don't feel deprived. I might not have had caramel apples, but I could always settle for a blackberry cobbler.

I do remember, however, how I would hang around while our cook was baking hoping for a handout. My persistence was often rewarded by my being treated to a few strips of leftover pie dough that had been first dusted with sugar, cinnamon, and a little grating of lemon rind and then baked along with what was in the oven. So don't discard any scraps of dough. Freeze them for a rainy day.

Interestingly, the one treat that practically every one of my friends mentioned was crispy marshmallow squares—something I had never tasted. And when we were making a version of these to be photographed, we had a hard time keeping the people working on this project from finishing off the batch before we could get a decent picture of them.

All the recipes included here are easy to prepare, which I suppose is one of the qualities that defines the category. And these recipes lend themselves to making substitutions and variations. If you don't have the ingredient called for, you can use something else. Who knows? When you come up with your own concoction, maybe it will be immortalized in some tot's mind, just as cane-syrup popcorn balls (page 158) are in mine, and crispy marshmallow squares (page 158) seem to be in everyone else's.

You can get really inventive by stirring together all sorts of leftovers. It's true that you could likely never reproduce exactly whatever wonderful invention you come up with, but that would be part of the fun. For instance, you could melt candy with a little liquid, stir in some nuts and crumbled cookies, and drop the mixture on wax paper by the spoonful. Or you could coat nuts and sprinkle them with cookie crumbs. Or you could mix everything with softened ice cream and refreeze it. Or you could stir leftovers into gelatin that has just about set. Some of these may not look so great, but the kids won't mind.

What hasn't been included, because not a soul mentioned them, is so-called health treats—things made of dried, unsweetened fruit and plain roasted nuts. But while you are in the inventing mood, this is certainly worth exploring. The trick is to make kids think they are getting something special or forbidden, not a food that is healthful. You can hit them later, after they are hooked, with the news that what they are eating is good for them. Such a ruse would probably have worked on me, anyway.

Then there is the question of a child's participation. Making a treat is a way to entertain kids when the weather or other circumstances have made it inconvenient or impossible to be outdoors. Concentrate on desserts that don't have to be cooked, such as the gelatin (page 158) or the chocolate cookie dessert (page 158). Recipes that require heating and melting ingredients are better done by an adult, leaving mixing, spreading, or making individual servings to the kids.

Another possibility is to let children make (or seem to make) a miniature batch of whatever you are preparing. Give them a small quantity of the recipe to stir or mix while you make the larger batch.

When ingredients must set or rest for fairly long periods, such as with the chocolate cookie dessert, be prepared with an interim treat to keep everyone quiet and satisfied.

I guess this is all pretty obvious, but it was a pleasure reconstructing and remembering the tastes in this chapter. And it was surprising how really tasty these treats were. We also had fun doing the photographs of the little girl, which introduces this chapter, as she tried to get at the just-out-of-reach popcorn ball. We talked it over and knew what kind of picture we hoped to get, but young Julia's determination and concentration were marvelous to watch. It was as if there wasn't another thing in the world as important as reaching that popcorn ball. At that particular moment, maybe there wasn't.

Incidentally, Julia is the daughter of Rochelle Udell and Doug Turshen, who designed this and my other books. Rochelle and Doug seem to think of everything, including having given birth to Julia just at the right time for her to be able to be a model later. Remarkable.

Brownie and Ice Cream Freeze

Brownie and ice cream freeze is the invention of Elizabeth Neidert. It's great because you can use all those bits and dabs of leftover ice cream you have in the freezer, and you can certainly substitute any soft cookie for the brownies.

      Brownies, cut up, or other kind of firm, dense cake
3 or more flavors of ice cream, slightly softened

Line a loaf pan with a piece of wax paper or cling wrap large enough so it will fold over the top when the pan is filled. Press a layer of ice cream in the bottom of the pan, smoothing over. Top this with with brownie pieces. Add another layer of ice cream and keep repeating layers until pan is filled. Smooth top and cover securely with cling wrap or wax paper. Allow to harden in the freezer.

    To serve, unmold (quickly run hot water over the bottom of the pan to loosen it) onto a serving plate and re-refrigerate for a few minutes or until set again. Slice and serve.

Serves 6 to 8 children

Stained Glass Gelatin

The best part of this dessert is that it looks so good and allows plenty of leeway in combining flavors.

    Of course, canned or fresh fruit can be stirred in when the gelatin is almost set, or you could stir it in when you mix in the cream.

5 flavors of packaged gelatin mix, such as lemon, lime, orange, wild cherry, and raspberry
1 cup heavy cream, whipped to soft peaks

Make the gelatin according to package directions but use only 1 cup boiling water and ½ cup cold water for each. Stir in the boiling water to thoroughly dissolve gelatin before adding the cold water. Place each in a separate round or square pan. Let set overnight or until firm.

    To assemble, cut gelatins into 1-inch cubes and remove from pans with a spatula. Layer cubes in a glass bowl and top with whipped cream. Or mix the cream with the cubes as you layer them.

    Refrigerate if not serving immediately.

Serves 8

Chocolate-Pecan-Raisin Clusters

You might just as easily make butterscotch walnut-raisin clusters as these chocolate pecan ones. To do so, substitute butterscotch morsels for the chocolate and walnuts for the pecans.

8 ounces semisweet or milk chocolate
¾ cup golden or dark raisins
¾ cup broken pecans or walnuts

Melt the chocolate in a saucepan over very low heat. Stir in the raisins and nuts. Drop in clusters on a sheet of wax paper. Allow to cool slightly, then chill to set chocolate.

Makes about 2 dozen

Chocolate Cookie Dessert

This dessert, made with chocolate wafers, is a variation on the one Nabisco calls famous chocolate refrigerator roll, printed on the back of their chocolate wafer package. It's a marvelous, easy-to-make dessert. Incidentally, I know a lot of adults who like it, too. You might make it for the grown-ups sometime (see the variation).

2 cups heavy cream
1½ teaspoons vanilla extract
2 tablespoons superfine sugar
1 package (8½ ounces) chocolate wafers

Whip the cream until soft peaks form, then stir in the vanilla and sugar. Continue whipping until stiff.

    Spread the cream generously on the chocolate wafers, then put wafers in stacks of 4 or 5. Arrange stacks lengthwise on a serving plate to make 1 long row.

    Frost the outside of the log with the remaining cream. Refrigerate for at least 3 hours (or overnight), or freeze until firm (covered with plastic wrap; let thaw in refrigerator 1 hour before serving).

    To serve, slice log on the diagonal.

Serves 6 to 8

Variation: Mix 3 tablespoons unsweetened cocoa powder into the cream along with the vanilla and sugar.

Grown-Up Variation: Omit the sugar and add 2 tablespoons framboise or other liqueur, or 2 tablespoons bourbon, to the vanilla and cream.

Clockwise, from above:
Freddie's Graham Cracker Pickups;
Stained Glass Gelatin;
Brownie and Ice Cream Freeze;
Chocolate-Pecan-Raisin Clusters;
Marshmallow-Butterscotch-Peanut Squares

Above: Chocolate Cookie Dessert
Below: Caramel Apples

Marshmallow-Butterscotch-Peanut Squares

This is a variation on everybody's favorite. They could probably be made with chocolate morsels instead of butterscotch, or you could make them as is and sprinkle chocolate morsels on top.

- 6 tablespoons (¾ stick) unsalted butter or margarine
- 10 ounces miniature marshmallows
- 6 cups crisped rice cereal
- 2 cups butterscotch morsels
- ¼ cup milk
- 1 cup honey-roasted peanuts

Butter a 13 x 9 x 2-inch baking pan and set aside.

Melt 4 tablespoons of the butter in a large saucepan. Add the marshmallows and cook over low heat until melted and smooth.

Off the heat, add the cereal, and stir to coat. Pat mixture into prepared pan. Set aside.

In another saucepan, melt the remaining butter and add the butterscotch morsels. Stir until soft, then add the milk, stirring until smooth. Mix in the peanuts and coat well. Pour evenly over the cereal and smooth top lightly.

Allow to set before cutting into squares.

Makes about 3 dozen

Caramel Apples

I'm sure there are a number of ways to make these, but part of the idea here is to do it the easiest way possible.

You might want to vary this by rolling the apples in chopped peanuts just before the caramel hardens.

- 1½ pounds caramels
- ⅓ cup evaporated milk
- 6 apples

Combine the caramels and milk in a large saucepan. Melt over low heat, stirring occasionally, until smooth and creamy.

Meanwhile, wash apples and spear each through the stem end with a small fork or sucker stick.

One at a time, stand apples in the melted caramel and spoon the sauce over to coat them completely. Let coated apples stand on a sheet of wax paper. When cooled, chill to set the caramel.

Makes 6

Freddie's Graham Cracker Pickups

This is a treat my remarkable Aunt Freddie came up with. I don't have any idea where she got the idea, but it is a surprisingly tasty combination of flavors.

- 24 whole graham crackers (48 squares)
- ½ cup (1 stick) unsalted butter, softened
- ½ cup sugar
- 1 cup coarsely chopped pecans

Preheat the oven to 350 degrees.

Arrange the crackers on a jelly-roll pan. Cream the butter and sugar until mixed, then stir in the pecans. Divide the mixture among the crackers and spread over each.

Bake for 12 to 14 minutes, or until melted and the color of maple syrup.

Let cool on a wire rack. Store in an airtight container.

Makes 2 dozen

Popcorn Balls

I think this is my favorite. I've always been hooked on popcorn, so popcorn balls are a natural for me. I also like Crackerjacks. You can add nuts to this, too.

- 3 quarts unsalted popcorn
- 2 cups cane syrup, dark corn syrup, or maple syrup
- 1 tablespoon cider vinegar
- ½ teaspoon salt
- 2 teaspoons vanilla extract

Place popcorn in a large bowl and set aside. Grease 2 large forks. Set aside.

Combine syrup, vinegar, and salt in a deep pot. (Pot must be deep because the syrup boils up and will overflow if not large enough.) Bring to a boil over medium heat until it reaches the hard-ball stage (250 degrees on a candy theremometer). Add the vanilla and mix well.

Pour over the popcorn and toss to coat with the greased forks. Butter your hands liberally and form popcorn into balls, pressing lightly to make them stick together. Continue forming balls, rebuttering your hands after each, until all the corn is used.

Makes about 1 dozen

Getting Ready

As with any other kitchen endeavor, the preparation of desserts is generally made easier by having the right equipment— "the right pot for the job." So if making desserts interests you, do a kitchen inventory and add the utensils you are missing. These items don't have to be bought all at once; instead, whenever you try a new recipe and find you're lacking something, add it then. By waiting until you actually need the item, you'll be less likely to buy things you can do without.

Of course, much basic equipment—sifters and rolling pins, for instance—does double duty and will already be part of your regular kitchen stock. But the assorted cake pans or tart rings are not usually there when you need them unless you've planned ahead.

Fortunately, none of this is too expensive, except for kitchen machines, such as food processors and ice-cream makers. Nowadays, good quality can be had at a fairly reasonable price. But just as top price does not always guarantee top quality, there is a price below which you really should not go. In the final analysis, you will just be wasting your budget if you are guided by cost alone. For example, pans that are too thin might be less expensive, but they will not bake as evenly and are more apt to bend out of shape. Strike a happy balance between price and quality.

And while you are thinking of what new things you might need, think also about how you are going to store them once you have them. I've found that one of the very best investments I've ever made in my kitchen was to have a section of lower cabinet shelves replaced with slots. This turned out to be a much more efficient use of space than the shelves that were there and it has made getting at the needed pieces infinitely easier. For years I had things stacked on top of one another, with what I wanted invariably on the bottom. When I corrected the situation, I was outdone with myself for not having gotten around to it sooner.

While I am all for improvising in a pinch, there are some things I am not willing to do without—a candy thermometer for instance, which renders candy and frosting making almost foolproof. In fact, I wouldn't make either frosting or candy without one. I'm sure professionals can wing it, but why should we if we don't have to? The cost of a single failure alone would pay for the thermometer, not to mention the frustration and mess of making a frosting that doesn't work.

Since one of the main, and very appealing, aspects of simple country desserts is their ease of preparation, there is not much in the way of fancy technique to master. Most of it you know already. And in the introductory remarks that open each chapter I try to touch on anything special that I think will make for better results. To tell the truth, there are not really many places you can go wrong on that score. Of course, we all occasionally overcook or scorch things, but that is not a matter of technique, but of attention to the task at hand. And even failures usually are not total. Anyway, some of this specialized equipment might prove not only to make you more efficient, but to provide an additional backup.

Incidentally, I'd buy *all* kitchen equipment in either white or stainless steel. Whenever you see terms like "decorator colors," run for the hills. And don't ever settle for those nasty noncolors like almond or harvest gold, or that god-awful pinkish tan. The only exception is with ceramic mixing bowls. These look good in natural glazed earth colors as well as classic white or cream. There is enough color pollution and color indecision around as it is; don't add to it in your kitchen.

Ice Cream and Ices

While I have fond memories from when I was a kid of turning the crank of the trusty old ice-cream maker, I don't think I would be so fond of doing the same thing now. As a matter of fact, I probably wouldn't bother to make ice cream today without some kind of automatic freezer. There are many different ones, but I have boiled the choices down to a few.

The other thing you often need, especially if you like custard ice cream, is a good double boiler. Anything else you might require will likely be found in your basic kitchen inventory or, if not, in the miscellaneous section at the end of this chapter.

*Simac Personal Ice-Cream Maker
This is really one of the best of the machines and has a built-in freezing unit. It is now available in a new smaller size, which makes it a space saver as well, and its performance is up to Simac's high standards.

One of the best improvements in the last few years is the advent of the removable canister. For a while companies were unable to master

the mechanics of separating the canister from the freezing unit without having to sacrifice efficiency and price. While having to clean a canister that was not removable was not as much trouble as it sounds it might be, the removable canisters makes things just that much easier.

*Gaggia Ice-Cream Maker
A wonderful machine that comes with two bowls so that you can make one batch, freeze it in the canister, and go directly into another batch. A very good product—as is everything from Gaggia.

*Donvier Ice-Cream Maker
This marvelously inventive little freezer is affordable to everyone. All you have to do is prefreeze the canister in your freezer. That's where it may be stored when not in use so it's always ready to go. Makes ice cream, sherbet, etc., with only a few easy turns of the handle on top.

**Zeroll dipper
Ice-cream dippers and scoops are much better than a spoon for serving (how many spoons have *you* bent getting rock-solid ice cream out of a carton?) These are well made of cast-aluminum. The dippers are filled with antifreeze so the metal is always warmer than the frozen dessert it goes into. Makes easy work of even very hard frozen ice cream. Well almost. Good "professional-looking" design as well.

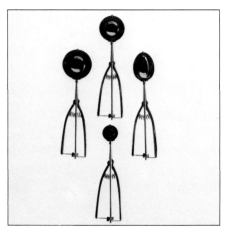

**Piazza scoops (Italy)
Made of stainless steel, these are high-quality and have a spring action. Available in a wide variety of sizes—from very small to truly huge. In oval shape, too.

**Flameprooof glass double boiler by Trans Duck

Double boilers come in all shapes and sizes. The weight of the material is important. This is an old standby, which is still one of the best if you want glass. Glass makes it possible to see how you are doing and to keep an eye on how rapidly the water is boiling.

**Copper and ceramic double boiler by Manviel (France)

Also a classic. Some people swear by them. The ceramic bowl is certainly efficient and easy to clean with its curved interior. If you don't mind a little extra weight (the ceramic insert is heavy) and cleaning copper, this might be for you.

**Brushed steel double boiler by Vollrath

I think of the three this is my favorite. It is heavy duty, and I like the very clean look of the design.

Cakes

If you are going to try your hand at cake making, by all means invest in some decent cake pans of varying sizes and designs. Bundt pans and tube pans are needed for fancy-looking cakes. And if you get serious, you might want a heavy-duty mixer, which is also good for mixing breads or other dense dough. This is a purchase you might delay until you determine just how serious you are. In any event, an electric hand mixer will certainly be handy, if not for mixing the batter then for making the cake icing.

There are also a couple of gadgets you might want to try, like cake strips and a cake tester.

**Heavy-duty mixer by KitchenAid

Almost all the enthusiastic cooks I asked rated the KitchenAid mixer as their first choice. And when it wasn't their first choice, it was always mentioned favorably. Good powerful motor, good bowls, and good looks.

**Hand mixers by Hamilton Beach and Krups

These are very handy for mixing light batters and whipping egg whites for icings. Look for a machine with a powerful motor and with blades that are easy to detach. You also want something that is neat and streamlined so it not only looks good but stores efficiently.

* *Available at Macy's and other department stores*
** *Available at Dean & DeLuca and other gourmet shops*
*** *Available at Lee Bailey at Saks Fifth Avenue and branches*

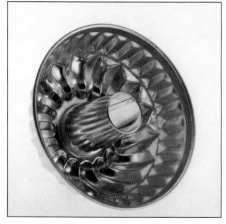

**Bundt pan by Kaiser

This kind of pan should be non-stick for easy removal. This is especially important in pans with a complicated design. Make sure they are made of heavy-duty aluminum, too, as this one is.

**Cake pans by Parrish's

You want heavy-duty metal here. Buy the professional weight if you come across it. This will help avoid warping and denting and will make for more uniform baking. If you have room to store them, buy a pair in several sizes and a pair of square pans as well.

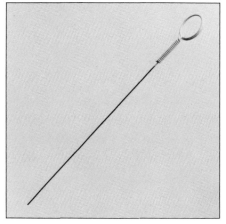

**Cake tester by Ateco

Frankly I use a clean straw from the whisk broom, but for those of you who feel this is not sanitary enough, this cake tester will do the trick. But you do need *something* to test the cake for doneness.

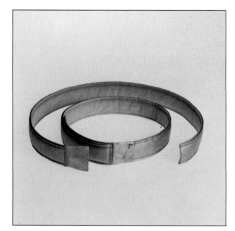

*Magic strips by J. T. Products

These little strips are soaked briefly in water before being pinned around the cake pan. This will keep the cake from forming a dome on top. Important for thick layers because a flat layer is easier to stack and ice.

*Mini-chopper by Cuisinart

I like this because it is very small, compact, and well-designed—also because it is easy to clean and use. Up to Cuisinart's high performance standards.

When mini-choppers first appeared they were just what the name implied: very small choppers for small-job use. But as always seems to happen with new products, manufacturers have not been content to let a good thing be. Instead they have tried to give the product additional features that are not necessary and are seldom used—in the process losing sight of the mini-chopper's original purpose. As a consequence, many so-called mini-choppers are now almost as big as the standard food processor and are really redundant.

**Tube pan by Hillside Metal

I'd invest in two sizes of these pans and try to have one with a removable bottom if possible. Non-stick is not as important a feature here as with the bundt.

Cookies

Everyone loves to make cookies. So get yourself some good sheets to bake them on, and if you want to make rolled-out cookies, you will need a good rolling pin and cutters.

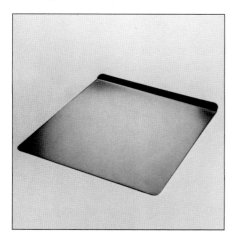

***Baking sheets by Cushionaire
To my way of thinking, these are the best. Because of their construction there is a layer of air between the top and bottom that allows even heat circulation and prevents hot spots. Also, they don't warp. The same company makes jelly-roll pans. I'd buy several in different sizes.

If you would rather have a thinner sheet, look for one with a non-stick surface that has enough weight to keep it from warping or bending and to distribute the heat evenly.

**Cookie cutters by Matfer (France)
The important quality to look for here is the sturdiness of the thin metal. You don't want a soft metal that will get out of shape. And, of course, a sharp edge is important. I'd buy several sizes. I like the ones with crimped edges, but this is purely aesthetic.

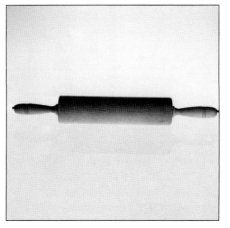

**Rolling pin by Thorpe
This is my choice because it is heavy and has a ball bearing that allows for even rolling out. The weight of the pin does some of the work for you.

Cobblers and the Like

You probably have everything you need to make these, except maybe for fruit corers —apple and pear.

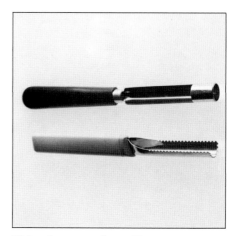

**Apple corer from France
These make the task of preparing the apples easier by getting rid of the core in one swift movement. What you want in an apple corer (or pear corer) is strength along with simple design.

***Pear corer from France
Same requirements as the apple corer.

*Available at Macy's and other department stores
**Available at Dean & DeLuca and other gourmet shops
***Available at Lee Bailey at Saks Fifth Avenue and branches

Candies

All the special equipment you need is the candy thermometer, which makes candy making accurate.

**Candy thermometer by Taylor
Sturdy construction with easy-to-read numerals.

Pies and Tarts

Pie-making, like cake-making, requires pans in various shapes and sizes. If you want to make pies or tarts that can be removed from their pans, look for pans with loose bottoms. There are now versions of glass pans that are non-stick, also helpful whether you want to remove the pie from the pan to serve it or not.

Although I'm certainly not suggesting you buy a food processor to make pie dough in, if you have one it will make your task easier. However, if you don't have a processor, I'd buy a pastry blender. It's a cheap tool and it makes blending much faster.

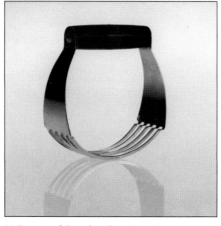

**Pastry blender by Fox Run
Heavy-duty metal with sharp edges and a good comfortable grip.

**Balloon whisk by Matfer (France)
I use a whisk to mix ingredients that need emulsifying and to stir custards. Purists use them to beat egg whites and to cream by hand. Suffice it to say, I am not a purist.

I might add that I think the balloon whisk is one of the most elegantly shaped pieces of kitchen equipment there is.

*Food processor by Cuisinart
The Cuisinart is the granddaddy of processors sold in America—and for my money still the best. I'd choose the DLC 7 Super Pro. All the attachments fit it, including the full set of blades—if you are interested. Has a good size work bowl.

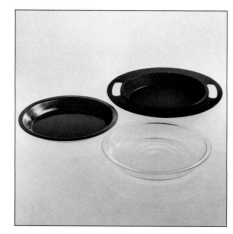

**Metal pie pans from France
If you prefer the old-fashioned kind of pie pan, buy heavy metal ones so they will retain their shape and bake evenly. Get them in several sizes.

*Pie pans with loose bottom by General Housewares
These are black steel with wide rims so you can make a larger crimp around the edges. The loose bottom allows a free-standing presentation. I like these because they have a sloping edge. Some loose bottom pans have a straight edge, which is not as deep or as graceful.

*Nonstick pie pans, "Clear Advantage" by Corning

This is a comparatively new product. If you like glass pans this should be your choice. I'd buy them in several sizes.

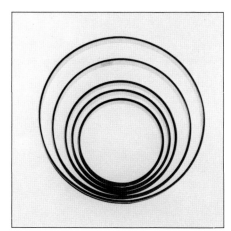

**Tart rings and squares from France

These are necessary for making some kinds of thin fruit tarts, which should be removed from the ring to serve properly. The rings and squares are simply placed on top of a heavy baking sheet when you use them. Heavy metal and assorted sizes are the requirements.

Fresh Fruit Desserts

Good sharp peelers and paring knives are important for preparing fresh fruit, but you probably already have those. However, what you might not have are zesters and strippers for citrus rind (I'm sure you have a grater).

Also, since some "composed" fresh fruit desserts use a dollop of purée or a sprinkling of chopped nuts, one of those new small "mini-choppers" comes in very handy.

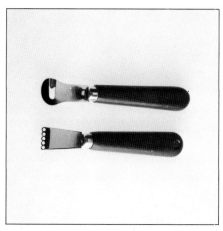

**Zesters and strippers from France

These are neat looking and have sharp edges, which are the qualities you're after. Buy them in several sizes so you can make zest and strips in a variety of thicknesses.

Coffee and Tea

To make these you need the proper pans and tins for the various kinds and shapes of cakes and muffins you might want to make.

**Muffin tins by Chicago Metallic

I like to have three sizes—giant, regular, and small—so that I am ready for all comers. These are heavy and bake evenly. I usually coat the insides with nonstick vegetable spray.

**Springform pans by Hillside

These are useful when you are making a cake that you want to remove easily from the pan. I use them often and have them in several sizes. These sometimes have a textured bottom.

---

*Available at Macy's and other department stores
**Available at Dean & DeLuca and other gourmet shops
***Available at Lee Bailey at Saks Fifth Avenue and branches

**Loaf pans by Guery (France)
Buy several sizes. Incidentally, Corning's nonstick "Clear Advantage" line also has loaf pans now if you want flameproof glass.

Puddings and Custards

What you need for pudding and custard making, besides a good double boiler (page 161), is an assortment of soufflé dishes and flan rings. You might also invest in antique molds when you see them. They are decorative (I used one to make the flans on page 68).

**Flan rings by Matfer (France)
These should be simple in design and come in several sizes.

**Soufflé dishes by Pillivuyt and Corning
Imported from France, the Pillivuyt porcelain soufflé dishes are widely available. They come in a good assortment of sizes. I would invest in a number of different ones, as well as individual dishes. The plain white ones are best.

If you want clear ovenproof glass, Corning is well designed and sturdy—and available all over the United States. Again, I would buy several sizes and individual ones too.

Miscellaneous

This category includes gadgets that you might already have as well as specialized utensils and equipment. Many of them may be used in making a number of the desserts mentioned above.

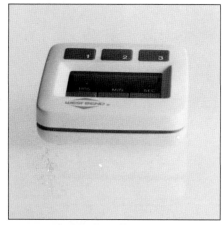

Timers by ***West Bend
I wish I liked the design and color of the West Bend product more than I do, but its triple function is so useful that I find it irresistible.

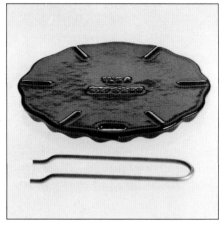

**Flame tamer by Ilsa (Italy)
A flame tamer is important to slow cooking and to keep things from burning.

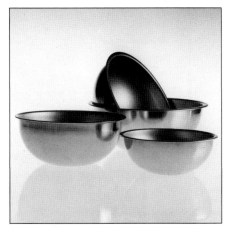

Mixing bowls by Vollrath (metal) and Pillivuyt (ceramic)

You will need several sets of these. I like to have a graduated set in heat proof glass as well as a set of the French-made ones. Metal and plastic bowls are also useful and are lightweight. Stackability is important, too.

Dry measuring cups by Foley

I use both glass and metal. Ideally they should stack into one another and be easy to read and store.

Liquid measuring cups by Anchor Hocking

Choose laboratory-type or good heat-proof glass with the same qualities of ease of reading and storability as the dry cups.

Measuring spoons by Foley

I have a number of sets of these so I don't have to keep washing and drying them to measure new ingredients. They should be on a ring so they don't all get separated. I like metal best.

*Available at Macy's and other department stores
**Available at Dean & DeLuca and other gourmet shops
***Available at Lee Bailey at Saks Fifth Avenue and branches*

Nutmeg grater by Marlux (France)

Freshly grated nutmeg is so much more flavorful than the ground nutmeg found on spice shelves that this is a worthwhile little investment. I use nutmeg in a number of desserts and maybe, if you don't already, you will when you get a grater, which is easy to use.

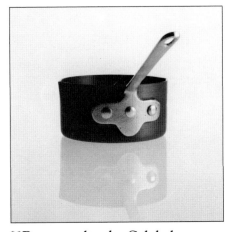

Butter melter by Calphalon

I know you can use a regular small pot for this job, but I find a very small saucepan with a little pouring spout is a very handy thing to have. Not just to use in making desserts, but for general cooking chores.

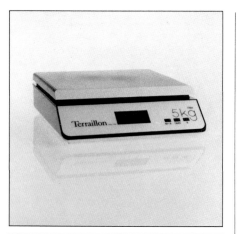

**Kitchen scales by Terraillon and Soehnle

I like both of these because of their design and accuracy. I use scales quite often because measuring by weight is so much more accurate.

**Oven thermometer by Taylor

You may not use this very often, but it is very useful when you need it. I check the accuracy of my ovens every so often to make sure they are not off.

**Wooden spoons from France

Another necessity as far as I'm concerned. I have them in all shapes and sizes. Choose good ones of smooth, well sanded, aged wood. The French-made ones are usually superior.

**Rubber spatulas from France

These are an absolute must. I seem to use them every time I cook —and probably so do you. If by some odd chance you don't have a set of them, run out now to buy one. Their handles should be of a good heavy-duty plastic or of wood, and the flat rubber end should be flexible. Rubbermaid also makes very good quality ones that are widely available.

**Sifter by Fox Run

The type with the flat triple screen in the bottom is my choice. I prefer the look of the larger ones with their big revolving hoops but, unfortunately, when they are full the hoops tend to throw the dry ingredients all over the place.

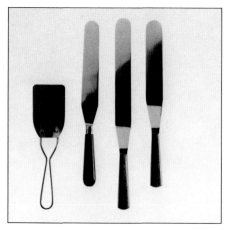

**Metal spatulas from France and the United States

These spatulas have a trim look and are of stainless steel. You should have several sizes and thicknesses, both flexible and rigid.

*Available at Macy's and other department stores
**Available at Dean & DeLuca and other gourmet shops
***Available at Lee Bailey at Saks Fifth Avenue and branches

Index

Conversion Chart
EQUIVALENT IMPERIAL AND METRIC MEASUREMENTS

American cooks use standard containers, the 8-ounce cup and a tablespoon that takes exactly 16 level fillings to fill that cup level. Measuring by cup makes it very difficult to give weight equivalents, as a cup of densely packed butter will weigh considerably more than a cup of flour. The easiest way therefore to deal with cup measurements in recipes is to take the amount by volume rather than by weight. Thus the equation reads:

1 cup = 240 ml = 8 fl. oz. $\frac{1}{2}$ cup = 120 ml = 4 fl. oz.

It is possible to buy a set of American cup measures in major stores around the world.

In the States, butter is often measured in sticks. One stick is the equivalent of 8 tablespoons. One tablespoon of butter is therefore the equivalent to $\frac{1}{2}$ ounce/15 grams.

Liquid Measures

Fluid Ounces	U.S.	Imperial	Milliliters
	1 teaspoon	1 teaspoon	5
$\frac{1}{4}$	2 teaspoons	1 dessert spoon	7
$\frac{1}{2}$	1 tablespoon	1 tablespoon	15
1	2 tablespoons	2 tablespoons	28
2	$\frac{1}{4}$ cup	4 tablespoons	56
4	$\frac{1}{2}$ cup or $\frac{1}{4}$ pint		110
5		$\frac{1}{4}$ pint or 1 gill	140
6	$\frac{3}{4}$ cup		170
8	1 cup or $\frac{1}{2}$ pint		225
9			250, $\frac{1}{4}$ liter
10	1$\frac{1}{4}$ cups	$\frac{1}{2}$ pint	280
12	1$\frac{1}{2}$ cups or $\frac{3}{4}$ pint		340
15		$\frac{3}{4}$ pint	420
16	2 cups or 1 pint		450
18	2$\frac{1}{4}$ cups		500, $\frac{1}{2}$ liter
20	2$\frac{1}{2}$ cups	1 pint	560
24	3 cups or 1$\frac{1}{2}$ pints		675
25		1$\frac{1}{4}$ pints	700
27	3$\frac{1}{2}$ cups		750
30	3$\frac{3}{4}$ cups	1$\frac{1}{2}$ pints	840
32	4 cups or 2 pints or 1 quart		900
35		1$\frac{3}{4}$ pints	980
36	4$\frac{1}{2}$ cups		1000, 1 liter
40	5 cups or 2$\frac{1}{2}$ pints	2 pints or 1 quart	1120
48	6 cups or 3 pints		1350
50		2$\frac{1}{2}$ pints	1400
60	7$\frac{1}{2}$ cups	3 pints	1680
64	8 cups or 4 pints or 2 quarts		1800
72	9 cups		2000, 2 liters

Solid Measures

U.S. and Imperial Measures		Metric Measures	
Ounces	Pounds	Grams	Kilos
1		28	
2		56	
3$\frac{1}{2}$		100	
4	$\frac{1}{4}$	112	
5		140	
6		168	
8	$\frac{1}{2}$	225	
9		250	$\frac{1}{4}$
12	$\frac{3}{4}$	340	
16	1	450	
18		500	$\frac{1}{2}$
20	1$\frac{1}{4}$	560	
24	1$\frac{1}{2}$	675	
27		750	$\frac{3}{4}$
28	1$\frac{3}{4}$	780	
32	2	900	
36	2$\frac{1}{4}$	1000	1
40	2$\frac{1}{2}$	1100	
48	3	1350	
54		1500	1$\frac{1}{2}$
64	4	1800	
72	4$\frac{1}{2}$	2000	2
80	5	2250	2$\frac{1}{4}$
90		2500	2$\frac{1}{2}$
100	6	2800	2$\frac{3}{4}$

Oven Temperature Equivalents

Fahrenheit	Celsius	Gas Mark	Description
225	110	$\frac{1}{4}$	Cool
250	130	$\frac{1}{2}$	
275	140	1	Very Slow
300	150	2	
325	170	3	Slow
350	180	4	Moderate
375	190	5	
400	200	6	Moderately Hot
425	220	7	Fairly Hot
450	230	8	Hot
475	240	9	Very Hot
500	250	10	Extremely Hot

EQUIVALENTS FOR INGREDIENTS

all-purpose flour—plain flour
cheesecloth—muslin
confectioners' sugar—icing sugar
cornstarch—cornflour
granulated sugar—caster sugar

shortening—white fat
sour cherry—morello cherry
unbleached flour—strong, white flour
vanilla bean—vanilla pod
zest—rind

light cream—single cream
heavy cream—double cream
half and half—12% fat milk
buttermilk—ordinary milk